Pitchin

WITHDRAWN

The Story of an
Early Illinois Colony,
Its Civil War Participation,
and a Family Remembrance

Charles M. Brock

ISBN-10: 1522765832
ISBN-13: 978-1522765837
Library of Congress Control Number: 2015920810
LCCN Imprint Name: CreateSpace Independent Publishing Platform,
North Charleston, SC

For Elizabeth
Fifty golden years and counting!

Acknowledgments

Special thanks to cousins Bill Borror and Doris Kogler, great-grandchildren of Silas Brock, for their patient guidance and insight.

A special thanks to the Iroquois County Genealogical Society in Watseka, Illinois, which continues to do an extraordinary job of collecting and cataloging documents and data. They are always extremely responsive and helpful.

I am grateful to the folks at the Archives of DePauw University and Indiana United Methodism, Greencastle, Indiana, for material relating to Indiana Asbury (now DePauw) University.

I have gathered many of the "Proceedings of the Reunions of the Society of the Survivors of the 76th Regiment, Illinois Infantry," from various sources:

(1) Champaign County Historical Archives, the Urbana Free Library, Urbana, Illinois
(2) Iroquois County Genealogical Society, Watseka, Illinois
(3) Kankakee County Museum Archival Collection, Kankakee, Illinois
(4) Local History and Genealogy Collection, Peoria Public Library, Peoria, Illinois

My thanks to all of those institutions.

Thanks to Mr. Towner Blackstock, Curator of Archives of The Fraternity of Phi Gamma Delta, for material regarding Marquis Lewis Brock. Thanks to the Virginia Historical Society for permission to use the map "Rebel Defences of Mobile," and to the Library of Virginia for permission to use the map of Fort Blakely, Alabama.

I have great affection for Watseka and for Iroquois County, where my brothers— Jim, Tom, and Steve—and I grew up. The four of us left many years ago to pursue dreams that our parents encouraged. My memories of a vibrant community remain vivid. Special thanks to my brothers for encouragement and wise counsel. Jim is an artist and author; Tom, a doctor; Steve, a professor of medieval philosophy.

This story relies on information from a number of sources in addition to the foregoing, including among others the 1880 *History of Iroquois County* by H. L. Beckwith, the Illinois State Archives, the National Archives, and the Library of Congress. I have strenuously endeavored to acknowledge sources of information and quotations. Any errors are unintentional and mine alone.

This is not a "top-down" professional history. It is a "bottom-up"—strictly amateur—family remembrance. If you prefer the former, you may skip directly to the family album in chapter 13.

The family in question is, of course, the Brock family, and its history in southern Indiana and Iroquois County, Illinois. As you will discover, that history cannot be fully understood except in the context of the lives of several other families, notably the family of Robert Morgan Roberts and in particular his two youngest sons, Bishop Robert Richford Roberts and Lewis Roberts. Accordingly, the story will begin with that family. A few details in the story reflect pure conjecture.

Tall ash tree fallen

across Mud Creek, grove standing

at attention. Old soldiers.

Town of Pitchin disappeared,

village vanished.

Pitchin Cemetery, graves

disintegrating,

left unattended.

Silent city.

Let silence speak!

Charles M. Brock

Contents

Introduction

I discovered the portrait of my paternal great-grandfather, Silas Brock, in the back of a closet in my mother's apartment. He is dressed in his Civil War uniform. Mother had no idea who did the painting. Nor could she tell me anything about his service. The subject of war was painful. Her brother Bill lost a leg in World War II, during the Normandy invasion in June 1944. Uncle Bill never spoke about that event, at least to me. With curiosity and concern, I saw him attach and remove his artificial leg, a clumsy contraption. He could throw a baseball with my brothers and me. But walking was always a struggle and a source of sadness for his parents and five sisters.

Apart from the war, my mother was happy to talk about Silas, his family, and their history in Iroquois County, Illinois, first in the rural area known as Ash Grove and the village of Glenwood, known as "Pitchin," and later in the town of Cissna Park. She showed me where Pitchin, now a ghost town, had existed. She took me to where Pitchin Cemetery, the burial ground for a number of my paternal ancestors, is located. Many of the tombstones in that cemetery are victims of time or vandalism or both; it has become difficult, in some cases impossible, to read their inscriptions. That visit to Pitchin came after my father died in 1999 at age ninety-two. I have no recollection of him ever taking me there or discussing its history.

My mother died in 2006 at eighty-nine. I retired from the practice of international law two years later.

After four decades of traveling the world, I have turned increasingly to family history. My father's files provided a bare-bones family tree as a starting point. Of course, in all fairness, he did not have access to the Internet.

The first part of this story focuses primarily on the Ash Grove area and certain farming families who colonized it, notably relatives and friends of Robert Richford Roberts, an early bishop of the Methodist Episcopal Church, and, of course, the Brock family, especially Silas.

Silas was born in 1841. He lived most of his life in the Ash Grove/Cissna Park area. He left for eighteen months, when his mother took him to study at Indiana Asbury (now DePauw) University in Greencastle, Putnam County, Indiana, and for three years, from 1862 to 1865, when he served in the Civil War as a soldier in the 76th Illinois Volunteer Infantry Regiment.

All of Silas and Maria's children were born and raised in Ash Grove. Their first child, a boy, died after ten days in September 1862, one month after Silas left for the war. The other four were born after the war.

Although Silas died in 1927, fourteen years before I was born, I feel that I know him. I knew two of his four children, Aunt May and Mark, my grandfather. And his ten grandchildren included my father Glen. I know him through family photographs. I know him from reading about the history of his regiment in the Civil War. I know him from my childhood in Iroquois County, where he lived most of his life. I do know Silas, but I would like to know him and the world he lived in much better.

Although I grew up twenty miles away, in Watseka, I never visited Pitchin or Pitchin Cemetery until after my father's death in 1999. It has haunted me ever since.

I have finally undertaken to write this story, after thinking about it for five or six years. I hope to bring Silas and his world into sharper focus through the prism of a prairie community, through its involvement in the Civil War, and through the lens of family memories.

If we listen intently, Silas might have something to say about the world we live in. But I'm getting ahead of myself. This story begins in 1833, eight years before Silas was born.

Cast of Characters

The principal characters in this story are numerous. Regarding the settlement and early development of Ash Grove, I have endeavored to focus on a few select individuals in addition to Bishop Roberts, Silas, and his wife Maria.

For the Roberts family:

Lewis Roberts, brother of the bishop

John Nunamaker, Lewis Roberts's son-in-law

John Hunnel, relative of Lewis Roberts's wife, Margaret Hunnel

John Willoughby, friend of the Roberts family and husband of Silas's aunt *Polly Brock*

For the Brock family:

Lewis Brock Sr., Silas's grandfather

Lewis R. Brock Jr., Silas's father

Mary Ann Bishop, Silas's mother

George Allen Brock, Silas's uncle

Nancy Brock, Silas's aunt and wife of Lewis Roberts's son *Jacob Roberts*

Wesley Harvey, nephew of Lewis Brock Sr.'s wife, *Mary Payne Richards,* and second husband of *Mary Ann Bishop*

See appendix 1 for partial family trees of the Roberts and extended Brock families. The primary source for the latter is Brock family history, including my father's files and information from Bill Borror and Doris Kogler. Bill's information includes several pages from Silas's Civil War diary.

Regarding the Civil War, the names are even more numerous. But my focus there is primarily the movement of Silas's regiment, the 76th Illinois, commanded for most of its existence by Col. Samuel Busey.   One exception to that focus is the court-martial of Truman Skeels, a cousin of Silas's, in another volunteer infantry regiment, the 113th Illinois.

Chapter 1
On the Lafayette-to-Ottawa Road in 1833

If you imagine a straight line from Lafayette, Tippecanoe County, in west-central Indiana to Ottawa, LaSalle County, in northern Illinois, it measures about 120 miles. That line cuts across Iroquois County in east-central Illinois. The following present-day maps of the contiguous states of Illinois and Indiana, with Illinois to the west, identify the locations of those counties, as well as several others that will figure in this story.

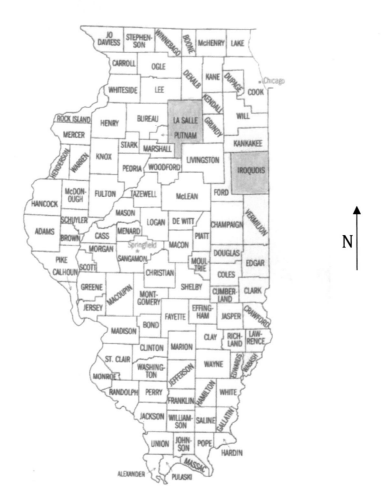

United States Census Bureau, Present-Day (2016) County Map of Illinois

United States Census Bureau
Present-Day (2016) County Map of Indiana

In the early 1830s, the old Lafayette-to-Ottawa dirt road was hardly a straight line, but it crossed the area that was to become Iroquois County formally in 1833. It was an ungraded pioneer road, seasonally muddy, dusty, or covered with snow, with ruts, rocks, and occasional tree stumps. It provided barely enough room for a wagon. But the rider on horseback could have a somewhat easier time, as long as he remained mindful of the dangers.

The road had no special name other than the Lafayette-to-Ottawa road, and no number. Nor does it exist today, having been replaced by a grid of state, county, and township roads.

"A Tree Planted by the Rivers of Water"

The rider reined his horse to a slow walk, as this particular stretch of road in Iroquois County was especially difficult. He was a tall, extraordinarily well-built man in his midfifties, with a high forehead and penetrating eyes. Although he was dressed in the plain clothing of a farmhand, it would have been readily apparent to anyone meeting and speaking with him that he was no ordinary individual.

The rider noted in particular the broad expanse of timber growing along the borders of the streams not far from the road, first Sugar Creek and then Mud Creek. Having spent all but his first seven years living in frontier wilderness, in western Pennsylvania and later in southern Indiana, he did not feel out of place in the prairie wilderness of central Illinois.

In the early 1820s, white visitors to the area that became Iroquois County were Indian traders employed by John Jacob Astor's American Fur Company, Gurdon Hubbard and Noel Vasseur. These men obtained furs from the Indians in exchange for goods. Hubbard established one of his trading posts in the northeast quarter of that area. The first permanent white settlements were established in 1830, one near Hubbard's trading post, and the other on Sugar Creek to the south. Hubbard closed his trading operations in 1834, by which time the Indians had been removed from the area.

The rider, Robert Richford Roberts, was an itinerant preacher and a bishop of the Methodist Episcopal Church, the creation of which John Wesley and others in England had inspired in the eighteenth century. Having left his Lawrence County home in southern Indiana several days before, Robert maneuvered his horse along this rugged road on his way to an important church meeting, the Rock River Conference, in northern Illinois. Already behind schedule, Robert vowed not to be late. He had ridden along Sugar Creek earlier in the day, and was now trekking the area that the Sugar Creek settlers referred to as Ash Grove.

Those settlers told Robert that the name "Ash Grove" came from a large ash tree in the woods next to Mud Creek. That ash, which had the distinction of being the only ash tree in the grove, had fallen across the creek. The grove was a sanctuary for travelers coming over the open prairie, which could be frightening because of winter storms and summer fires.

In the waning dusk, Robert began searching for a suitable spot to take refuge for the night. This was 1833 and Iroquois County was a wild and swampy prairie except for forested areas along the rivers and creeks. Deer, wolves, and wild hogs wandered freely. Rattlesnakes, mosquitoes, and greenhead flies infested the tall grass. Fortunately, the road to Ottawa ran not far from Mud Creek and the thick timber that hugged its banks.

As Robert made camp for the night, his thoughts turned from his conference duties to what lay around him—the grove, Mud Creek, and the prairie nearby and beyond. Not a soul in sight—no log houses, no plowed fields, no cattle or oxen—only the tall prairie grass stretching to the horizon and the narrow road running through it. He heard the distant howl of a timber wolf.

Beginning around 1830, farmers from Indiana and elsewhere had settled the area along Sugar Creek, some ten miles east of where Robert tethered his horse for the night. Earlier that day, he saw one of those settlers, John Hunnel, a farmer who had moved from Lawrence County, Indiana in the fall of 1830. John was related to Margaret Hunnel, the wife of Robert's younger brother, Lewis.

John spoke highly of the fertility of the prairie soil near Sugar Creek and the settlement known as Milford. He said settlers were beginning to buy large tracts of prairie land. Early on, the settlers had believed the prairie was not fit for cultivation, but that notion was soon discredited. On the contrary, the rich black soil under the tall grass was proving to be exceptional for farming. John warned Robert that drainage was a problem, given the area's "swampiness."

The conversation with John planted a seed in Robert's mind. He had traveled this way before, but the possibility of a farming opportunity in the area for his family had not occurred to him until now. He knew the federal government was offering public domain land for sale here at $1.25 per acre. As he knelt for evening prayer, he recalled the third verse of Psalms 1: "And he shall be like a tree planted by the rivers of water, that bringeth forth his fruit in his season; his leaf also shall not wither; and whatsoever he doeth shall prosper."

Preaching to the Trees

Robert Richford Roberts was born on a small farm in Frederick County, Maryland, in 1778. His ancestors, of Welsh origin, had originally settled on Maryland's Eastern Shore. His father's name was Robert Morgan Roberts. To avoid confusion, I will refer to his father as Robert Sr. and to him as Robert Jr.

Robert Sr. fought in the Revolutionary War. After the war, he acquired some four hundred acres of public domain land from the state of Pennsylvania in the Ligonier Valley east of Pittsburg. He probably received a government warrant to acquire the land by virtue of his war service.

Robert Sr.'s future in Maryland was limited because his father's land descended to his oldest brother pursuant to the law of primogeniture. So in 1785, Robert Sr. decided to make his own opportunity in the frontier wilderness of Western Pennsylvania. That area was by then considered safe from Indians. He migrated with his family, which then included ten children. The four youngest were Robert Jr., who was seven; Lewis, five; Priscilla, two; and Nancy, six months.

In 1794, Robert Jr. joined the Methodist society, as it was then called. His parents had been members of the Church of England when they lived in Maryland. He found himself drawn to the spiritual life and to evangelical preaching; living in the wilderness, he practiced by preaching to the trees. But a decision to make the itinerant ministry a vocation did not occur for some time.

Worth Tippy's biography of Robert Jr., *Frontier Bishop*, says that by the mid-1790s, he had developed an intensely strong desire to strike out on his own. Pennsylvania was opening land for settlement in the Shenango Valley, a hundred miles to the north of the Ligonier Valley toward Lake Erie. "Settlers were offered four hundred acres of land at twenty dollars for each hundred acres, on condition that a cabin be built and twenty-five acres be brought under cultivation within five years" (Tippy 1958, 40). Although Robert Jr.

was not yet of age, after much discussion he finally received permission from his father to accompany several other young men, including Robert Jr.'s older brother Thomas, to Shenango, to stake out claims. Robert Jr. staked out a claim with financial help from his father and built a crude log cabin. Eventually, his father, his brothers Thomas and Lewis, and his older sister Elizabeth migrated from Ligonier Valley to Shenango to join him. The other children remained in Ligonier.

Robert Jr. met Elizabeth Oldham in the Ligonier Valley, and they married in January 1799. She was born in 1776 and came from York, Pennsylvania. For the young couple's honeymoon journey, they made a five-day trip on horseback through the snow-covered mountainous wilderness from Ligonier Valley to Robert Jr.'s log cabin in Shenango.

After they married, the two of them struggled with the question of whether he should take up the itinerant ministry as a vocation. It would mean long periods of travel on the Methodist circuits for him, long periods of separation for the two of them, as well as an uncertain financial future. However, after considerable discussion, they concluded that Robert Jr. should enter the ministry. He was admitted to the Baltimore Conference of the church in 1802, ordained a deacon in 1804, and made an elder in 1806.

Lewis Roberts, Robert Jr.'s younger brother, joined the Methodist society, following his older brother's example. Unlike Robert Jr., however, Lewis continued the life of a frontier farmer in Shenango. There he met and married Margaret Hunnel, who had been born around 1776.

Migration to Indiana

Members of Margaret's family emigrated to southern Indiana, and they reported that the land there was more fertile and less crowded than that in Shenango. In 1811, Lewis, Margaret, and their six children left Shenango. They eventually settled in the wilderness of southern Indiana, on the East Fork of the White River. The Indiana frontier attracted Lewis, given the increasing population in western Pennsylvania—people coming across the Appalachian Mountains in search of opportunity. Both he and Robert Jr. were frontiersmen at heart, and they would remain so all their lives. The area where Lewis and Margaret settled in Indiana became the southeastern corner of Lawrence County.

One of Lewis's younger sisters, Priscilla, married a farmer named James Chess in the Ligonier Valley. Lewis and Priscilla, two years apart, had always been close, so it was not surprising that Priscilla, James, and their two children, Ellenor and James Jr., migrated with Lewis from Pennsylvania to Indiana.

Robert Jr. visited his siblings and their families once they had settled in southern Indiana. He looked over the area, and he liked what he saw. The public domain land in the area of the East Fork of the White River had been surveyed pursuant to the federal government's Public Land Survey System and was open for settlement. I will explain that Survey System in more detail in relation to Ash Grove.

In 1816, Robert Jr. was elected bishop of the Methodist Church. Three years later, he and Elizabeth left Pennsylvania for Indiana and settled in a log cabin near Lewis. They had no children. Robert Jr. had a particular interest in extending the reach of Methodism in the South, and westward to the Mississippi River and beyond, and Lawrence County was more conveniently located than Pennsylvania to accomplish that purpose.

In 1821, Lewis's daughter, Catharine, married John Nunamaker. He was born in 1798 in Jefferson County, Kentucky, according to one source. Sometime in the late 1820s, John established a pottery business in Lawrence County. He developed a close relationship with his father-in-law, Lewis, both of them being frontiersmen. Catharine and John had at least nine children. The first, born in 1823, was named Lewis, after her father. The sixth, John Wesley Nunamaker, was born in 1834, the year the family migrated to Ash Grove. The latter fought for the Union army in the Civil War.

Lewis Roberts purchased land in Lawrence County in 1821. He also began a long-term interest in public service, becoming a justice of the peace in 1823. While a justice of the peace was not required to be a lawyer, he typically heard minor criminal cases and small claims proceedings, and he performed civil marriage ceremonies.

Lewis became a member of the Indiana House of Representatives in 1826 for a two-year term.   One John Brown, who alleged that Lewis had won the election by only three votes, and that nine of the votes cast were illegal, contested Lewis's election to the House. The Committee on Elections concluded that the contest of Lewis's election was supported by sufficient evidence, and that Brown was entitled to a seat in the General Assembly. However, the House rejected the recommendation of the committee, and voted 44 to 12 to retain Lewis as a member. He was appointed to the Standing Committee on Roads.

Roberts/Brock Wedding

Sometime between 1810 and 1812, Lewis Brock and his wife Mary Payne Richards emigrated from Tennessee to what would become the northwestern part of Washington County, Indiana, in search of farmland. That heavily forested area was contiguous with what became the southeastern corner of Lawrence County. Like Robert Jr. and Lewis Roberts, Lewis Brock was a frontiersman, moving ahead of the country's ever-increasing population. Lewis and Mary Brock had at least nine children, including Nancy (1803), Elizabeth (1806), George Allen (1809), twins Gabriel and Margaret (1811), Polly (1818), Rachel (1821), Lewis R. (1823), and Minerva (1826). According to family history, Lewis Brock, whose ancestry was English, was born in Knox County, Tennessee, in 1783.

In 1820, Lewis Roberts's second son, Jacob, who was born in Shenango in 1801, married Nancy Brock, Lewis and Mary Brock's oldest child. Their marriage was quite significant, because this Roberts/Brock union was the catalyst that eventually brought my ancestors to Iroquois County, as I will explain later.

Nancy and Jacob had at least ten children. The four who appear in this story are John L. and Thomas H., both of whom served in the Union army in the Civil War, and two daughters, Matilda and Elizabeth.

One of Lewis Brock's children, Lewis R. Brock, was Silas's father.

What the middle initial "R" in his name stood for remains unknown. His mother's maiden name was Richards, so his middle name may have been Richards. For purposes of clarity in this story, I will use a senior/junior designation: "Lewis Sr." was Silas's grandfather and "Lewis Jr." Silas's father.

Chapter 2

Early Settlement of the Ash Grove Frontier, 1834–1835

Public Land Survey System

In Robert Jr.'s journey through Ash Grove in 1833, he camped for the night near where Mud Creek meets Pigeon Creek. Property that included or at least bordered the stream and timber would, he thought, be ideal for settlement. John Hunnel said that, as far as he knew, no one had yet purchased land in the Ash Grove area. That, he told Robert Jr., would have to be verified.

Robert Jr. envisioned a village near the creek, with a chapel and parsonage. As he settled down for the night, he imagined the invisible straight lines—intersecting north/south and east/west lines—of the Public Land Survey System crossing the creek, running through the trees and over the prairie. Those survey lines were used to measure and locate public domain acreage available for sale. The federal District Land Office in Danville, in adjacent Vermilion County, handled sales of such land in Iroquois County.

The following map from H. W. Beckwith's *History of Iroquois County* displays the lines and section numbers created in the area of Ash Grove (as configured in 1880) by the Survey System. The area that I have shaded in green plays a central role in this story (Beckwith 1880, I: 260).

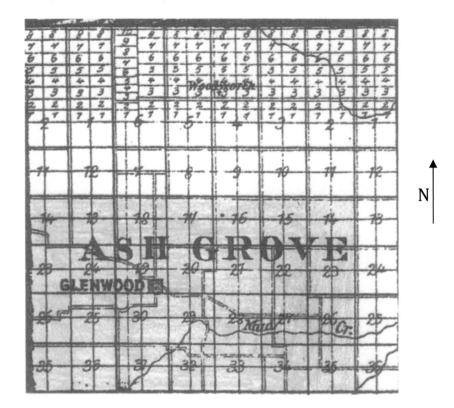

N

Focusing on the green-shaded area, each numbered "section" is approximately one square mile and contains 640 acres. The system provides for subdivision of a section into partial sections—quarter sections, half-quarter sections, quarter-quarter sections, etc.

This map identifies the location of the village of Glenwood. The area's residents generally referred to that village, which no longer exists, as "Pitchin."

The representation of Mud Creek on this map is incomplete. The creek runs west from Section 29 through Sections 30, 19, 24, and 23. (Refer to the maps in chapter 3 for a more complete representation.) The irregular line that runs southwest from Section 29 through Section 31 and 32 is Pigeon Creek.

Two unusual features of this map may be ignored for present purposes: first, the irregularly shaped sections in the northern third of the map, and second, the duplication of section numbers between the two north-south tiers of sections on the west side of the map and the two tiers of sections on the east side of the map. An explanation of those peculiarities would add unnecessary complexity to the story.

The Founders of Ash Grove

Whatever Robert Jr. said to his brother Lewis when he returned to Lawrence County from the church conference was ultimately persuasive. No doubt, Lewis's dislike of the growing population in Lawrence County played a role. In 1820, that population was about 4,100; by 1830, it had more than doubled to 9,200. Also, by 1834, the Potawatomi and Kickapoo Indians were removed from the area of east-central Illinois.

In 1834, Lewis bought public domain land crossed by Mud Creek, and he migrated to Ash Grove with his son-in-law John Nunamaker, his daughter Catharine's husband. Lewis purchased two 80-acre tracts on May 1 in Section 28 from the Danville Land Office. The two men built the first dwelling in Ash Grove, an eighteen-by-twenty-foot log cabin on the bank of the creek.

Beckwith's *History* asserts that Robert Jr. was the first purchaser of public domain land in the Ash Grove area, in 1833. But I have found no evidence of that in the Illinois State Archives, or in the General Land Office Records of the Bureau of Land Management, US Department of the Interior. Those sources point to Lewis Roberts as the first purchaser, in 1834, perhaps with funds supplied by Robert Jr. I have found no evidence that Robert Jr. purchased land in Ash Grove in his own name from the government in 1833. Those sources reflect purchases by Robert Jr. of 200 public domain acres in November 1835 and November 1836.

In any event, Beckwith names Lewis Roberts as the first white settler and the "father" of Ash Grove. In addition to the 160 acres he purchased in 1834, Lewis also acquired 120 acres, again in Section 28, in 1836 and 1837, resulting in a substantial farm of almost half a section. As you will recall, a full section encompasses 640 acres.

My view is that Robert Jr. should share with Lewis the distinction of being the founders of Ash Grove, given the former's vision of a farming community and given the assistance that he apparently provided to his brother Lewis and others to make that vision a reality. However, Robert Jr. never moved from Lawrence County to the Ash Grove area. He was simply too preoccupied with church matters. From 1834 to 1836, he served as presiding bishop of the Indiana Conference of the church. He also became one of the founders of Indiana Asbury (now DePauw) University in Greencastle, Putnam County, Indiana, in 1837. In the years before his death in 1843, he was almost continuously on the road, not only in Indiana and Illinois but throughout the country.

Federal Land Patent dated October 20, 1835

(Cited as "United States Department of the Interior, Bureau of Land Management"
in the bibliography)

Federal Land Patents

Purchasers of public domain land received federal land patents evidencing their ownership. For example, the patent on the previous page was issued to Lewis ("Louis") Roberts with respect to his purchase on May 1, 1834, of one of the two 80-acre tracts in Section 28. It states that he was then a resident of Lawrence County, Indiana, so he made the purchase in anticipation of his move to Ash Grove. The patent was signed on behalf of President Andrew Jackson on October 20 "in the year of our Lord one thousand eight hundred and thirty five and of the Independence of the United States the sixtieth." There was often a delay between the actual purchase and the issuance of the patent.

You will note the operative words in the patent reflect purchase of "the South Half of the South West quarter of Section Twenty Eight." In other words, Lewis acquired one-half of one-fourth of 640 acres (that is, 80 acres). "Township Twenty Five North of Range Thirteen West" names the coordinates of the Survey System, which identifies the Ash Grove area by reference to an east/west "base line" in southern Illinois and a north/south "meridian line" in central Indiana. I don't propose in this book to explain the Survey System in more detail, as it would add a level of complexity unnecessary for the story. If you are interested, you may refer to the excellent work by Ralph and Virginia Moore, published by the Iroquois County Historical Society in 1977, or to the Illinois Public Domain Land Tract Sales Database in the State Archives of the Illinois Secretary of State.

Other Early Settlers

John Hunnel moved to Ash Grove from Sugar Creek in 1834, shortly after Lewis Roberts and John Nunamaker. Hunnel purchased 80 acres in October and December 1834, thus being the second land purchaser in Ash Grove. He bought an additional 120 acres in 1836.

John Nunamaker bought 40 acres in 1835, and an additional 40 acres in 1841; then John's wife, Catharine, purchased 40 acres in 1842. For a number of years, Nunamaker and his sons continued the pottery business that he had started in Lawrence County. He later constructed a mill on his property.

Chapter 3

Later Arrivals, 1836–1855

Roberts Family and Friends

Robert Jr.'s envisioned colony in Ash Grove expanded considerably after 1835. Purchases by family and friends from Lawrence County between 1834 and 1855 totaled 2,904 acres of public domain land. See the chart in appendix 2 for a summary, prioritized by date of first purchase. To put that expansion into perspective, recall that one standard section of land in the Survey System contains 640 acres, or one square mile. So their purchases were equivalent to 4.5 sections, or 4.5 square miles.

The map on the following page focuses on certain sections in the Ash Grove area where those purchases were made. This map and the Ash Grove maps that follow are derived from the extraordinary work of Ralph and Virginia Moore. The underlying map is theirs; the coloring is mine. The tracts colored in red are those purchased by individuals from Lawrence County between 1834 and 1855 (except for the tract bought by Samuel Wesley Jenkins,

just south of Section 31 in what was then part of Ash Grove). Eighty percent of this land was purchased from the Danville Land Office for $1.25 per acre (in one case $0.50 per acre), and 20 percent was acquired using federal land warrants.

Under federal statutes, the government granted bounty land to certain veterans of military service, such as veterans of the War of 1812 and the Mexican War. Recipients used government-issued land warrants instead of cash to pay for the land. In a number of cases, veterans or their heirs sold the warrants rather than use them to acquire bounty land. Those sales were private transactions so the Illinois State Archives do not indicate the prices paid for such warrants. In the late 1840s and 1850s, the government assigned certain tracts to members of the Ash Grove colony based on such land warrants.

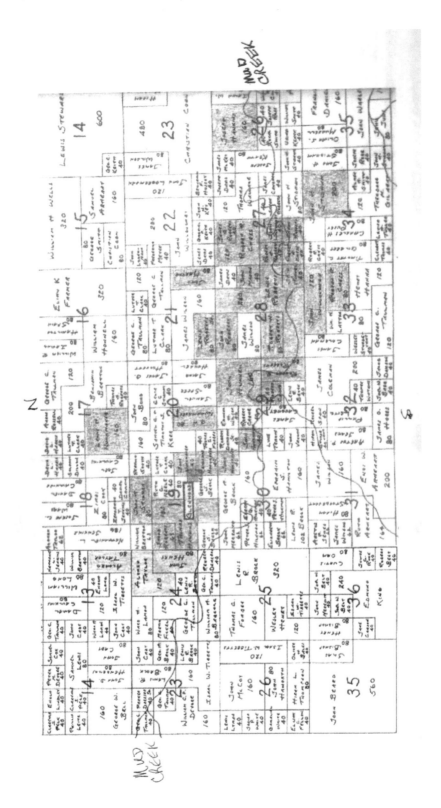

Extended Brock Family (Brock, Harvey, and Bishop Families) and John Cady Family

Lewis Roberts told his son Jacob of Robert Jr.'s idea of establishing a colony in Illinois. Both father and uncle encouraged Jacob to join. However, his wife, Nancy, was reluctant to leave her family. Jacob thought that her father, Lewis Brock Sr., might be interested. At age fifty he was initially reluctant to uproot his family again. Nevertheless, following the departures of Lewis Roberts and others in 1834 and 1835, given encouragement by Robert Jr., and hearing reports about the fertility of the Ash Grove soil, Lewis Brock Sr. had second thoughts. He was also concerned about the growing population in Washington County. The federal census, which was 9,000 in 1820, grew to 15,300 by 1840.

In 1836, Lewis Brock Sr. acquired public domain land in Ash Grove from the Danville Land Office. In 1837, he and his wife and six of their nine children resettled in Iroquois County. Her father's move helped to convince Nancy, so Jacob Roberts purchased public domain land in Ash Grove in 1837.

One of Lewis Brock Sr.'s children who made the move to Illinois was Lewis Jr. Mary Ann Bishop arrived from Ross County, Ohio, in 1839 with her brothers Silas and George Bishop. Lewis Jr. and Mary Ann married in 1840. The couple would become Silas Brock's parents.

Another child of Lewis Sr. who came to Illinois in 1837, from White County, Indiana, was George Allen Brock. He had married Elizabeth Harvey, the sister of Wesley Harvey, in Washington County. They made the trip to Ash Grove with an ox team.

Wesley Harvey was born in 1821 on a farm near Salem in Washington County, the third of four children of Robert and Sally Richards. His father was born in North Carolina, but he moved to Tennessee at an early age. About 1810, Robert and his family moved to Indiana. Wesley was a nephew of Lewis Brock Sr.'s wife, Mary Payne Richards.

Wesley's mother died when he was three. He lived with several relatives, including Lewis Sr. and Mary, until he was twelve, when he set out on his own. He worked as a farmhand for $3.50 to $6.00 per month. Eventually he moved to White County to live with his sister Elizabeth and George Allen Brock. He emigrated with them to Ash Grove in 1837 at about the same time that Lewis Sr. moved there from Washington County. Wesley lived with the Brock family in Ash Grove until 1841, when he married his first wife, Mary Henry, a daughter of John Henry. Lewis Roberts, who was then justice of the peace, performed the wedding ceremony.

Polly, the sixth child of Lewis Brock Sr., also came with the family to Illinois. In 1838, she married John Willoughby, a friend of the Roberts family from Lawrence County. More about Polly and John later.

In all, six of Lewis Sr.'s nine children moved permanently with him to Illinois. His daughter Elizabeth had died in 1833, at age twenty-seven.   That left only the twins, Gabriel and Margaret, who were twenty-six and who chose to remain in Washington County.

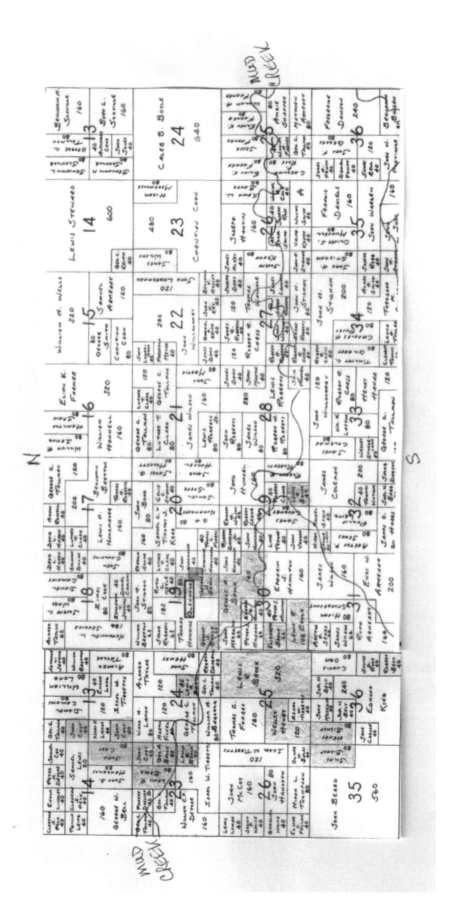

Land Purchases by the Extended Brock Family

The map on the preceding page focuses on certain sections in the southern half of Ash Grove where the extended Brock family and the John Cady family established themselves. I will recount the history of John Cady later. The tracts colored in blue are public domain land (or Illinois Central Railroad land, which I will explain in due course) that was purchased by extended Brock family members, and the tracts colored in yellow are those of John Cady. All the land purchased by Lewis Brock Sr. and Lewis R. Brock Jr. is designated as that of Lewis Jr. on the map. Following is a summary of those purchases.

Brock Land Purchases

Before bringing his family to Iroquois County, Lewis Sr. purchased 80 acres of public domain land in the Ash Grove area in May 1836 from the Danville, Illinois, Land Office. That 80-acre tract was located in Section 23 at the head of the grove, and was crossed at its southern end by Mud Creek. Lewis Sr. paid $100, or $1.25 per acre, for the 80 acres.

When the Brocks arrived in 1837, they built an eighteen-by-twenty-foot log cabin as a temporary shelter just north of their 80 acres, on land they did not own, in Section 14. Then, in 1838, they built a permanent home on the 80-acre homestead, after clearing timber. Silas was born there on December 12, 1841.

Lewis Sr. purchased an additional 40 acres in 1838 (in what is present-day Artesia Township, just west of Ash Grove) and another 40 acres in 1839 in Ash Grove, not far from the original 80-acre homestead, all for $1.25 per acre. He would ultimately receive federal land patent documents for all three tracts. Following is a summary:

Lewis Sr.'s Cash Purchases

DATE OF PUBLIC DOMAIN LAND PURCHASE	TRACT SIZE	PURCHASE PRICE	DATE OF ISSUANCE OF FEDERAL LAND PATENT DOCUMENT
May 16, 1836	**80 acres**	**$100**	**November 1, 1839**
September 6, 1838	**40 acres (Artesia Township)**	**$50**	**October 10, 1840**
September 12, 1839	**40 acres**	**$50**	**August 1, 1842**
TOTAL	**160 acres**	**$200**	

Lewis Jr. purchased public domain land in the 1850s as summarized in the following table. The first and third of those tracts were located in present-day Ash Grove, the second in the Loda area, southwest of Ash Grove:

Lewis Jr.'s Cash Purchases

DATE OF PUBLIC DOMAIN LAND PURCHASE	TRACT SIZE	PURCHASE PRICE	DATE OF ISSUANCE OF FEDERAL LAND PATENT DOCUMENT
May 24, 1850	**40 acres**	**$50**	**December 2, 1850**
July 18, 1853	**40 acres (Loda)**	**$100**	**March 1, 1855**
November 22, 1854	**120 acres (2 lots, 80 and 40 acres)**	**$60**	**April 15, 1857**
TOTAL	**200 acres**	**$210**	

In the 1850s the government assigned certain public domain tracts to Lewis Jr. based on transferred land warrants, all in Ash Grove except as noted:

Lewis Jr.'s Purchases by Warrant

DATE OF ASSIGNMENT	TRACT SIZE	PURCHASE PRICE	DATE OF ISSUANCE OF FEDERAL LAND PATENT DOCUMENT
December 8, 1852	**80 acres**	**Land Warrant**	**January 2, 1854**
December 8, 1852	**40 acres**	**Land Warrant**	**January 2, 1854**
June 2, 1853	**40 acres**	**Land Warrant**	**October 2, 1854**
July 18, 1853	**40 acres**	**Land Warrant (Loda)**	**October 2, 1854**
July 18, 1853	**40 acres**	**Land Warrant (Loda)**	**October 2, 1854**
July 18, 1853	**40 acres**	**Land Warrant**	**October 2, 1854**
TOTAL	**280 acres**		

Finally, Lewis Jr. also acquired two tracts in Ash Grove in Section 30 from the Illinois Central Railroad on August

8, 1854, one of 62 acres and the other 40 acres, for $2.50 per acre.

In summary, Lewis Sr. purchased 160 acres between 1836 and 1839. Lewis Jr. purchased 582 acres between 1850 and 1854.

Sale of Original Homestead; Creation of New Homestead

It appears from Iroquois County Circuit Court files that, in 1845, three months before his death, Lewis Sr. divided the original Brock homestead purchased in 1836 and sold the north half (40 acres) to Wesley Harvey. In 1849, Lewis Jr. sold the south half to one Isaac Tibbets.

At the time of that sale to Tibbets, Lewis Jr. owned 120 acres in Section 23, 80 acres acquired as public domain land and 40 acres acquired from his brother George Allen. The sale to Tibbets covered all 120 acres, not just the south half of the homestead. The purchase price for the 120 acres was $1,000, with $550 payable upfront, and the remaining $450 payable in five annual installments, with payment being secured by a mortgage. The unusual feature of the transaction was that the $450 was payable in "good shop-made boots" at $3 per pair. After Lewis Jr.'s death, Wesley Harvey, as the executor of his estate (see Chapter 5), acknowledged in writing that the debt had been paid in full. I assume Tibbets did not deliver 150 pairs of boots to Lewis Jr. I assume that payment was made, in the words of the mortgage, "according to the true intent and meaning thereof." The record is silent as to that intent.

Between December 1852 and November 1854, Lewis Jr. purchased 320 acres in one section of Ash Grove (Section 25), southwest of Pitchin. Those were the four land warrant purchases in Ash Grove and the November 22, 1854, purchase of 120 acres, referred to in the foregoing charts. In addition, the 102 acres he purchased from the railroad on August 8, 1854, were contiguous to the 320-acre site, in Section 30 south of Pitchin. In other words, he consciously set out to create a substantial farm, and he succeeded in doing that over a two-year period. That farm became his new home. I mention this here also because the 320-acre segment of that farm played a significant role in the lives of Lewis Jr.'s children after his untimely death in 1855.

George Allen Brock's and Elizabeth Harvey's Land Purchases

George Allen Brock and his wife, Elizabeth Harvey, acquired 405 acres of public domain land in Ash Grove between 1837 and 1842, all at $1.25 per acre.

Wesley Harvey's Land Purchases

As previously mentioned, Wesley bought the north half of the Brock homestead in Section 23 in 1845. He later bought the Nunamaker farm in Section 19. Between 1852 and 1854, he purchased 160 acres of public domain land in Section 25. The map incorrectly names the owner of those 160 acres as "Wesley Henry."

The chart in appendix 3 summarizes the purchases of public domain/Illinois Central Railroad land by members of the extended Brock family, including the Harveys, prioritized by date of first purchase. Private land transactions, such as those of Wesley Harvey just mentioned, were numerous, but are not included in either appendix 2 or appendix 3.

John Cady Family

According to Beckwith's *History*, John Cady came to Ash Grove from Lawrence County, Indiana. (Another source says he came from Owen County, Indiana.) However, because of the unusual nature of his story, I am treating him separately rather than in the earlier section regarding the Roberts family and friends.

Beckwith cites the story of John Cady as an example of one who lost property by not purchasing land through the Land Office. That's not the entire picture. Cady, about age forty, came to Ash Grove in 1837 "with a yoke of oxen and a team of horses hitched to the same wagon."

He arrived soon after the Lewis Brock Sr. family. Like Lewis Sr., he purchased land through the Land Office in 1836, before he left Indiana—40 acres in the northeast corner of Section 23, adjoining the Brock homestead—for $1.25 per acre. Also like the Brocks, when he first arrived he built a temporary shelter just north of those 40 acres on land that he did not then own, in Section 14. Unlike the Brocks, however, he did not move onto his purchased property the following year. Rather, he decided to remain in Section 14, where he built a permanent home and grew an orchard. Perhaps clearing the timber in Section 23 was too much of an effort. In any event, I assume he did not have the money to pay the government for additional land. I also assume that he believed he could rely on the notion of "squatters' rights" to stay on Section 14. What he did not anticipate was the eventual coming of the railroad.

The Illinois Central Railroad was incorporated by statute in February 1851, and the State donated to it a considerable amount of land, including the land in Section 14 on which Cady had established his home and orchard. The railroad's sales of such land (including the sale to Lewis Jr. noted earlier) enabled it to generate funds to help defray the cost of railroad construction. Cady did not have the $2.50 per acre necessary under the statute to pay the railroad in order to exercise the statutory "right to purchase," so he was forced to sell his home and orchard.

In 1852 and 1853, Cady bought 80 acres in Section 13, using federal land warrants. According to Beckwith, he built a new home in Section 13. Then in 1854, he bought from the railroad the 80 acres in Section 14 on which he had built his original home.

A footnote to the foregoing regarding the "right to purchase" under the 1851 statute: As indicated earlier, Lewis Jr. purchased 102 acres from the Illinois Central Railroad in August 1854 for $2.50 per acre. As required by the statute, he represented (1) that he was the owner of an improvement on that land made prior to September 20, 1850, (2) that the improvement was intended as a residence or for agricultural purposes, and (3) that he had filed with the clerk of the Iroquois County Circuit Court the necessary notice and affidavits.

According to the 1860 census (where his surname is misspelled "Rady"), Cady and his wife, Ellen, had three sons living with them—Robert (twenty-three), Thomas T. (twenty), and David (ten). The census raises a question about a fourth son named John, age twenty-six. But, according to another source, their son John Wesley Cady died at the age of ten, and he is buried in Pitchin Cemetery. Thomas Cady served in the Union army in the Civil War.

The Roberts/Brock/Cady Colony

Although Beckwith's *History* does not say so, I believe it is credible to treat the Roberts family and friends, the extended Brock family, and the John Cady family as members of one colony. Expanding the scope of the colony to include the 1,587 acres acquired by the Brocks and John Cady meant 4,491 acres purchased by colony members between 1834 and 1855, equivalent to seven sections, an impressive number— 25 percent of the total land area on the map on the following page. That map shows the combined purchases of the Roberts family and friends (red), the extended Brock family (blue), and John Cady (yellow) summarized above, mostly hugging the grove and Mud Creek.

Would the Brock family have moved to Ash Grove from Indiana if the Roberts family had not led the way? It seems unlikely, but I have no objective proof one way or the other.

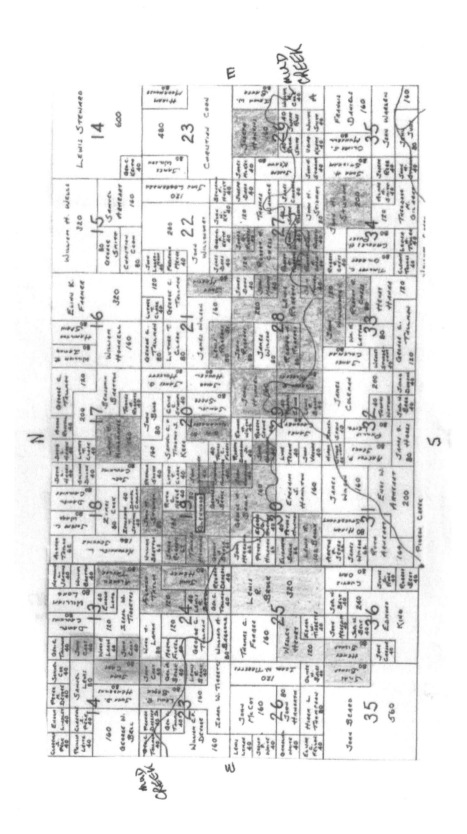

Chapter 4

From Colony to Community— Leading Citizens of Early Ash Grove

Ash Grove evolved gradually in the 1830s and 1840s into a community, as families continued to arrive from Ohio, Indiana and elsewhere. Land was cleared and cultivated. Farmers eventually produced more than they needed locally, and began looking to marketplaces in Chicago and Lafayette, Indiana, to sell their produce. A village started up, and a schoolhouse was built. Lewis Roberts and his family and friends in particular were instrumental in developing the community.

Lewis Roberts and Margaret Hunnel

Already a substantial landowner by 1837, Lewis Roberts farmed his 280 acres in Section 28. He also farmed the adjoining land of his brother the bishop, who, as I said before, never moved to Illinois. Lewis Roberts continued his commitment to public service by becoming the first Ash Grove justice of the peace, as he had done in Lawrence County. Beckwith's *History* tells the story of how he handled the office:

> It was an old saying of his that as long as he was justice of the peace that portion of Iroquois county should never be disgraced with a lawsuit; so, true to his word, as soon as any person would come to him entertaining the idea of commencing suit, the argument would begin, not, as in these days, after the testimony was in, but immediately, Roberts

trying to effect a compromise. Sometimes two whole days would be occupied in obtaining a settlement. But it is said he never failed in making both parties satisfied; for at the expiration of his term there had not been a single suit in the town. In marrying parties he always collected the legal fee, but directly handed it over to the bride, be it a large or a small amount, as a wedding present. Mr. [Wesley] Harvey's first wife [Mary Henry] was the recipient of the fee, as was Rachel Brock [Silas Brock's aunt], when she married Orvis Skeels, it being the second wedding in the township (Beckwith 1880, II: 650).

Blessed are the peacemakers.

Rachel and Orvis Skeels were the parents of Truman Skeels, who served in the Union army in the Civil War.

As Beckwith notes, Lewis Roberts also had a passion for politics. As he had done in Indiana, he became a member of the state legislature—the Illinois House of Representatives—in 1838 for a two-year term.

Roberts's first session in the House was held in Vandalia, Fayette County, Illinois, where the state capitol was located until 1839, when it was moved to Springfield. That term was also Abraham Lincoln's third of four terms in the Illinois House. Lincoln was defeated in his bid to become Speaker of the House in December 1838. After four vote counts, with Lewis Roberts voting for Lincoln, one William Ewing was finally elected Speaker. Lincoln was appointed to the Standing Committee on Finance, Roberts to the Standing Committee on Salines. The latter committee concerned itself with the sale of saline lands (salt springs or salt works) in several counties, including Vermilion County.

In February 1839, Roberts procured the passage of a law providing for the relocation of the county seat (then called the "seat of justice") of Iroquois County from Montgomery (now the town of Iroquois) to a more central location. In June of that year, the county commissioners appointed for that purpose decided upon Middleport, now Watseka, as the site for the county seat.

Beckwith also recites an anecdote from Roberts's term in the Illinois legislature:

> After a tedious morning session of the legislature spent in the discussion of some political measure they adjourned for dinner, Lincoln dining with his friend Roberts. No sooner had they seated themselves at the table than the discussion was resumed, in which the honorable member from Iroquois so far forgot himself as to reach and help himself to meat three or four times in succession. Upon noticing this Mr. Lincoln reached and took a piece from Mr. Roberts' plate. This attracted his attention and he immediately demanded an explanation, asking if he intended to insult him. Lincoln immediately and very courteously begged pardon, saying, "Excuse me; I took yours for

the meat plate." Great laughter ensued at Mr. Roberts' expense, who soon saw what was the matter (Beckwith 1880, II: 643).

Lewis Roberts, like Lincoln, was a member of the Whig Party, as were all the men of Ash Grove. In the 1840 presidential election, they all voted for the Whig candidate, William Henry Harrison ("Tippecanoe and Tyler Too"). General Harrison won the election, but died of pneumonia one month after inauguration.

John Nunamaker and Catharine Roberts

In 1835, Lewis Roberts's daughter Catharine and son-in-law John Nunamaker built a house on their land in Section 19, about a mile north of Mud Creek. That was the first building in what would become the village of Glenwood, or Pitchin. Nunamaker set up a kiln and continued the pottery business that he had begun in Lawrence County—in Beckwith's words, "the manufactory of crocks, jugs, churns and dishes of clay." (Beckwith 1880, II: 644) After four or five years, he started a sawmill. In the early 1850s, Nunamaker opened a small mercantile business.

Nunamaker's activities decided the location of Pitchin. It evolved and grew in the years that followed, turning the vision that Robert Jr. had in 1833 of a village in Ash Grove into a reality. The following present-day (2016) map of Iroquois County, in which I have highlighted Ash Grove, shows where Pitchin was located:

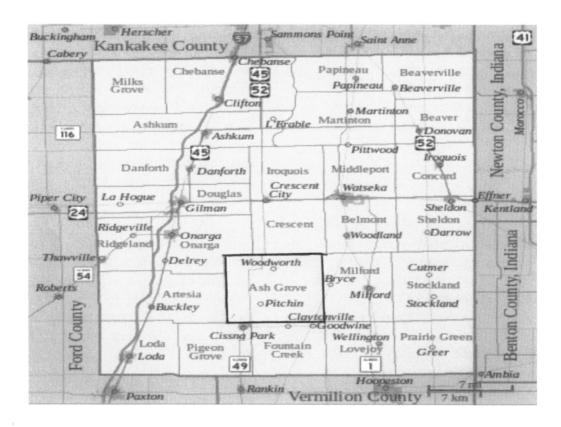

(Cited as "Map of Iroquois County [Current]" in the bibliography)

According to the Iroquois County Genealogical Society, "the name [Pitchin] derives from the following legend: 'Two of the town's residents got into an argument which led to a street fight. As the fight was progressing, a crowd began gathering. An old woman who was among the observers urged those close to "pitch-in." They did and a free-for-all began. Afterwards the incident was referred to as "the pitch-in" and became the nickname of the town.'" (Iroquois County Cemetery Project: Ash Grove Twp. Cemeteries).

But another reason for the name may also be possible. When I was a child, we frequently had potluck dinners at the Watseka Methodist Church, meaning meals where each person or family attending contributed a dish. In some places, such as southern Indiana—which is where the colony families came from—such a meal is referred to as a "pitch-in." For example, in September 2014, the Cavetown Cemetery Board in Campbellsburg, Washington County, Indiana announced its annual meeting to be held on September 28 at the Cavetown Church, with a "pitch-in" meal at 1:00 p.m. Was that expression common two hundred years ago? I don't know. Could that have been the derivation of the nickname of the village—collaboration rather than conflict? Perhaps, but I think the free-for-all meaning is more likely.

Again according to the Iroquois County Genealogical Society, "in the 1800s the town consisted of a Methodist church, a 14 room hotel, a general store, a drug store, a variety store, doctor's office, blacksmith shop, three carpenter shops, a school house and 20+ homes. Today less than half a dozen houses remain" (Iroquois County Cemetery Project: Ash Grove Twp. Cemeteries). The hotel was named Grand Pacific. At its peak, Pitchin had about 150 inhabitants.

Bishop Roberts's vision of a chapel and parsonage in Ash Grove did not materialize for some years. Initially church meetings were held in private homes, the first being the home of Lewis Roberts, and the second the original Brock homestead. Beckwith says that a Methodist parsonage was built in 1851 or 1852, and that two Methodist chapels, the Wesley and Flowers chapels, were built in 1855:

> These are credited as being the first frame churches erected in the county. The cause of building these two places of worship was not on account of any "split" among the members, but on account of the creek [Mud Creek]. Those on the south side claimed they could not attend church all the time on account of the distance and high water, while those on the north side, through priority of settlement, claimed the right to build north of the stream. Accordingly, in the spring of 1855 each faction commenced a church. That on the south side, under the name of Wesley chapel, was first to be commenced, but the one on the north side the first to be completed (Beckwith 1880, II: 654–655).

In 1853, John and Catharine Roberts Nunamaker transferred certain property in the southeast corner of Section 19 into a trust for the construction of a Methodist church and parsonage. The trustees were James Calman [Coleman], John Stidham, Robert R. Roberts (a son of Lewis Roberts), Lewis R. Brock Jr., Alonzo Taylor, and Lewis Nunamaker (a son of John Nunamaker). However, Beckwith says that the Flowers chapel was originally built in Section 24 on an acre of land contributed by Alonzo Taylor, and moved in 1868 into the village.

As to the Wesley chapel, south of Mud Creek, it might have been built on land donated by Isaac Tibbetts in the northeast corner of Section 26. James Coleman, a minister, and three other men hauled the lumber to build it from Boone County, Indiana, one hundred miles away.

Sometime after 1853, the Nunamakers left Ash Grove and moved to Bernadotte, Fulton County, Illinois. Some believe their decision to move resulted from the increasing population of Iroquois County. According to the 1840 federal census, the county then had only 1,695 inhabitants—on average, about one person per square mile. By 1850, it had increased to 4,100. Then came the railroad—the Illinois Central Railroad—in 1853–1854, which ran from Chicago through Iroquois County. By 1860, the population had tripled to 12,300.

On the other hand, as of 1850, the population of Fulton County was 22,500. So the primary reason for the Nunamakers' departure from Ash Grove was not population. Rather, their son John Wesley Nunamaker, a farmer, moved in the 1850s to Fulton County, and they joined him.

Lewis Roberts Jr.

In 1841, one of Lewis Roberts's sons, Lewis Roberts Jr., taught the first session in the first schoolhouse in Ash Grove. The schoolhouse was a log cabin with slab seats and greased-paper windows. It operated on a subscription basis, with each family paying the teacher directly ($1.50 per student). School sessions were three months long, with all grades together in one room. Mary and Marquis Lewis Brock, children of George Allen Brock and Elizabeth Harvey, attended school in that schoolhouse. Silas Brock began his education there. Later the people of Ash Grove established the Glenwood School, a public school.

McGuffey's Eclectic Readers were popular in nineteenth-century grade schools. The schoolteachers in Ash Grove, as elsewhere, taught the three R's—reading, writing, and arithmetic— as well as history and geography. They also taught basic values, such as fairness, honesty, and punctuality.

Lewis Roberts Jr. went on to become a Methodist minister, and he moved to Peru, Miami County, Indiana.

Glenwood School, which became school district 180 in 1887

John Willoughby and Polly Brock

Beckwith tells the story of John Willoughby, who was born in 1808. When he was young, the overseer of the poor in Lawrence County, Indiana, indentured him to Bishop Roberts. But the bishop treated him as one of the family, offering him the opportunity to emigrate to Ash Grove. Willoughby did so in 1838. There he married Lewis R. Brock Jr.'s sister Polly.

Beckwith also recounts in detail the story of a trip in June 1842 by John Willoughby, Lewis R. Brock Jr., and Wesley Harvey to deliver their produce to market in Chicago—thirteen bushels of wheat, thirty bushels of corn, and a few hundred pounds of bacon. They sold the wheat for $0.85 per bushel, corn for $0.30 per bushel, and bacon for $2.50 per hundred pounds. The one-hundred-mile trip by oxen-drawn wagons took about ten days (Beckwith 1880, II: 647-648).

Willoughby would eventually become a substantial landowner in Ash Grove between 1869 and 1874.

More about these three men later.

John Hunnel and Jane Hunnel

The people of Ash Grove established the village cemetery, known as Glenwood or Pitchin Cemetery (or Ash Grove Cemetery), in 1842 on land in the northeast quarter of Section 29, near the fork of Mud Creek and Pigeon Creek, donated by John Hunnel. The first person to be buried there was Daniel Farris, who died in June 1842 at age forty-two, survived by his wife, Sarah, and four children, ages nine, seven, six, and one. His wife later remarried and moved to Shelby County, Indiana. His youngest son, George Ferris, served in the 51st Indiana Volunteer Infantry Regiment, Company I, during the Civil War.

A number of Roberts family members and friends are buried in Pitchin Cemetery, along with a number of Silas Brock's extended family members. (See appendix 4.)

Pitchin Cemetery was not a private family cemetery. It was "the principal 'silent city' of the town...on the shady and grassy bank of the creek, containing about three acres" (Beckwith 1880, II: 653).

Chapter 5

A Siege of Untimely Deaths:
1843–1855

Robert Richford Roberts, Lewis Roberts, Margaret Hunnel, and Nancy Brock

On his way to the Rock River Conference in northern Illinois in the summer of 1842, Bishop Roberts made one last visit to Ash Grove to see his brother Lewis. He preached a sermon near the grove with Ecclesiastes 11:1 as his text: "Cast thy bread upon the waters: for thou shalt find it after many days."

Bishop Roberts died in 1843 at age sixty-four in Lawrence County. His wife Elizabeth died in 1858. Both are buried on the DePauw University campus in Greencastle, Putnam County, Indiana.

Lewis Roberts died in Ash Grove in 1848 at sixty-seven, and Margaret died in 1849. They are buried in Pitchin Cemetery.

The question is what impact did those deaths have on the viability of the community? What did the other people listed in appendix 2 do after those deaths? There were essentially two groups—the first, those who purchased land between 1834 and 1842; the second, those who purchased later, in 1847 and beyond. The first group made no additional land purchases, while the second continued to make substantial purchases. It appears the deaths of the bishop and Lewis Roberts had a significant impact on those who migrated early to Ash Grove with Lewis Roberts. One exception was John Willoughby, who remained in Ash Grove and made substantial land purchases between 1849 and 1874.

Jacob Roberts's wife, Nancy Brock, died in January 1844 in Ash Grove. Their youngest child, Elizabeth, had died after ten days in September 1843. Sometime after Jacob's father died in 1848, he and his children returned to southern Indiana. He remarried there, to Rosannah Thompson, and they had four children. Jacob died in Washington County in 1859.

Lewis Brock Sr., George Allen Brock, Lewis R. Brock Jr., Polly Brock, and Rachel Brock

Between 1845 and 1855, Lewis Brock Sr., George Allen Brock, Lewis R. Brock Jr., Polly Brock, and Rachel Brock died. All except Rachel are buried in Pitchin Cemetery. I have not been able to identify Rachel's place of burial.

Lewis Brock Sr. Lewis Sr. died intestate (without a will) in 1845 at age sixty-two. One asset of Lewis Sr.'s estate was the south half (40 acres) of the Brock homestead in Section 23. As you will recall, Lewis Sr. sold the north half of the homestead to Wesley Harvey in 1845. In 1846, George Allen Brock, as administrator of Lewis Sr.'s estate, petitioned the Iroquois County Circuit Court to appoint a guardian for Lewis Sr.'s minor heirs, and to order division or sale of the south 40 acres for the benefit of those heirs. The commissioners the court appointed to partition the land in question (Lewis Roberts, Wesley Harvey, and Samuel Wesley Jenkins) concluded that an equitable division was not possible. Accordingly, the court ordered Wesley Harvey to cause the property to be sold at public sale for the benefit of the heirs. He held a public auction in August 1848, and Lewis Jr.'s bid of $38 was the winning bid. The tract was transferred to Lewis Jr. in March 1849. As noted in Chapter 3, Lewis Jr. then sold it to Isaac Tibbets.

George Allen Brock. George Allen Brock died in 1849 at age forty, leaving five minor children—Mary, Marquis Lewis, Robert W., William, and Sarah. (The records do not indicate what the "W" in Robert's name stood for. Perhaps "Wesley"?) George Allen's wife, Elizabeth, and her brother Wesley Harvey were appointed guardians of the children.

George Allen's will, which named Wesley as executor, made provision ($500) for support of William, who was severely mentally retarded, but it made no provision for the support and education of the others. The guardians requested an order from the Iroquois County Circuit Court to allow them to sell two items of residential real estate near Pitchin, and to utilize the proceeds for the support and education of the other children.

According to the Iroquois County Genealogical Society case file, George Allen had intended to move from Ash Grove to Greencastle, Indiana, to provide a good education for his children, because "there are no suitable schools in the neighborhood where the…infants reside."

The guardians were not able to sell the property privately, so they asked the court to authorize a public auction, with the purchaser to sign a five-year note secured by a mortgage. The land was worth about $7 per acre. Lewis Jr. was the highest bidder at the auction. He paid $300 for the property.

Lewis R. Brock Jr. Lewis Jr. died on November 8, 1855, at thirty-two. His wife, Mary Ann, was only thirty-three and Silas thirteen. According to family lore, Lewis Jr. got caught in a storm and contracted pneumonia. His will, dated three months before his death, acknowledged that he was in poor health. It named Wesley Harvey as executor. It instructed the executor to sell all of Lewis Jr.'s real estate, except for certain specified tracts, as soon as it would bring $12 per acre.

The tracts exempt from sale by the executor were the *north half* of the 320-acre farm southwest of Pitchin, and 32 residential acres in the area where Pitchin was located. Mary Ann was to have the use of those two tracts unless she should remarry.

The will also instructed the executor to sell personal property not necessary on the farm, and to pay the estate's debts. Mary Ann was to have all remaining money derived from the sale of Lewis Jr.'s property necessary for the support and education of the family. But if she should remarry, she would receive just $400 in cash; the remainder of his estate would be shared equally among their four children—Silas, Charles,

Hannah and Sarah. (A fifth child, a girl, had died in infancy.)

Wesley caused the remaining nonexempt real estate, including the *south half* of the 320-acre tract and the land that Lewis Jr. had acquired from the Illinois Central Railroad, to be sold for $50.

But in December 1858, the four children became undivided joint owners also of the *south half* of the 320-acre tract. "Undivided" means that the four children held title without specifying the interest of each child by percentage or description. They now owned the entire 320-acre tract that Lewis Jr. had purchased and developed. They also acquired an additional 10 residential acres in the Pitchin area. It is unclear how they were able to arrange those acquisitions.

The story of the 320-acre farm is continued in Chapter 7.

Polly Brock. The wife of John Willoughby, Polly Brock died in 1854 at age thirty-six. Their son, Winfield Scott Willoughby, served in the Union army in the Civil War. Her husband continued farming in Ash Grove for many years.

Rachel Brock. Rachel Brock married Orvis Skeels, but he died in 1841, and she died in 1855 at age thirty-four. Their son, Truman Skeels, served in the Union army in the Civil War, and he was court-martialed in 1864.

Footnote: Of the six children of Lewis Brock Sr. and Mary Richards who moved permanently with them to Iroquois County, Minerva is not included in this story because she married and moved away from Ash Grove. She also died very young, at age twenty-four. Regarding the twins, who remained in Washington County, Margaret died in 1845 at age thirty-four, and Gabriel died in 1859 at age forty-eight. Gabriel was the only one of the nine children of Lewis Sr. and Mary Richards to live past the age of forty.

Lewis Roberts

Lewis Brock Sr.

George Allen Brock

Lewis R. Brock Jr.

Polly Brock, wife of John Willoughby

Chapter 6

Indiana Asbury (now DePauw) University (Greencastle, Putnam County, Indiana)

As already noted, Bishop Roberts was one of the founders of Indiana Asbury (now DePauw) University in 1837. It was named in honor of Bishop Francis Asbury, the first American bishop of the Methodist Episcopal Church. "To this institution he [Bishop Roberts] gave major effort during the last ten years of his life, and he made it the residuary legatee of his estate" (Tippy 1958, 172).

Several individuals from the Roberts and Brock families, including Silas, attended the university at various times and for various periods.

John L. Roberts

DePauw's records list John L. Roberts from Washington County, Indiana, the oldest son of Jacob Roberts and Nancy Brock, and Silas's first cousin, as a student at Indiana Asbury in 1852. He did not graduate.

Roberts farmed in Lawrence County, and married Laura Ann Edwards there in 1856. They had three children. In 1863, he enlisted in the 117th Indiana Volunteer Infantry Regiment, Company H, for a six-month term. John and Laura's daughter Mary Jane died in 1869 at age nine; sometime thereafter, the family moved to Neosho County in southeast Kansas.

Marquis Lewis Brock

As it turned out, George Allen Brock's wish to see his children educated in Greencastle came true in part. Two of his children, Marquis Lewis and Robert W., went to Greencastle—to Indiana Asbury University.

Marquis Lewis was born in 1835 in White County, Indiana, where his parents were living before emigrating to Ash Grove in 1837. He was a member of the Indiana Asbury class of 1856, in the Classical Department, where he received a bachelor's degree. He was also a member of Phi Gamma Delta fraternity. Marquis Lewis tutored at the university in 1856. In 1859, he received a master's degree without further study, since the university did not then offer graduate courses.

From 1858 to 1869, Marquis Lewis was an instructor at the Illinois Institute for Education of Deaf and Dumb in Jacksonville, Illinois. His story continues in chapter 12.

Silas Brock and Robert W. Brock

After the death of his father, Silas, at thirteen, had no choice but to take on significant responsibility for running the family farm. However, as his health was poor, his mother took him at age fifteen to Indiana Asbury University.

The tuition in the Preparatory Department was $7 per three-month term, and $10 per term in the Collegiate and Scientific Departments.   The janitor fee was $1.50 per term, and the library fee was $0.50 per term. The university made no provision for boarding students. Boarding was readily available with families at prices ranging from $1.50 to $3.00 per week. Many students found rooms on their own or, as in Silas's case, with family members. Students had to supply their own books. "As a general estimate, it may be stated that the whole expense of a young man in the University need not exceed from $150 to $200 per annum. All above the latter amount, it is believed, is very generally worse than thrown away" (Indiana Asbury University catalog, 1856–57).

DePauw's records show both Silas and his cousin Robert W. Brock enrolled in the "Normal Class" for the academic year 1856–57, the same year that Marquis Lewis was engaged by the university as a tutor.

This material is courtesy of the Archives of DePauw University and Indiana United Methodism, Greencastle, Indiana.

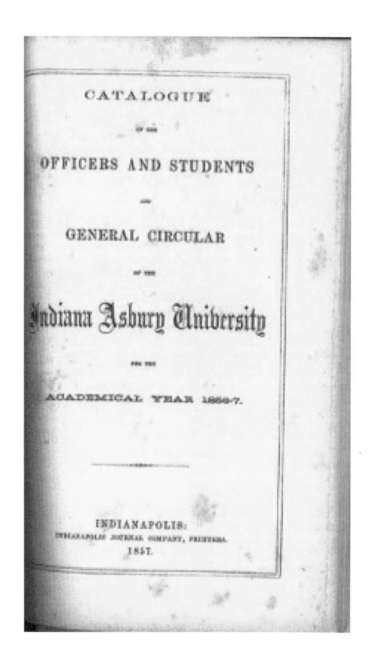

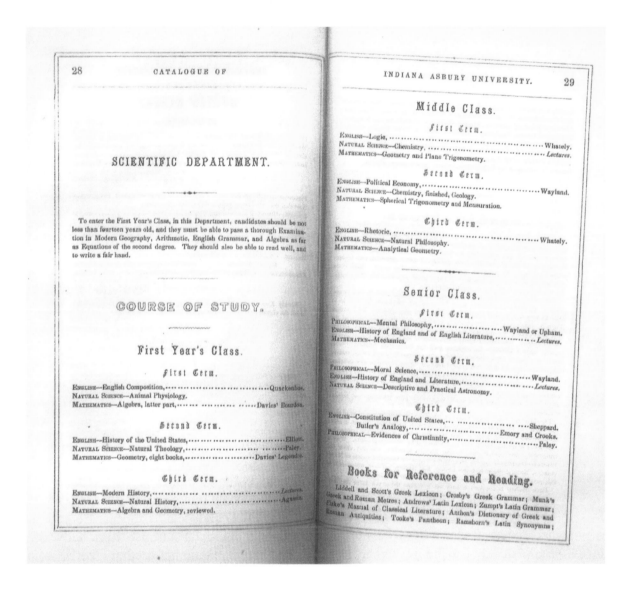

The records also show Silas enrolled in the "Scientific Department" as a first-year student in 1857–58. But Silas did not graduate. In fact he may not have finished the first year in the Scientific Department. The demands of the farm required him to cut his education short.

DePauw's records show Robert W. Brock entered the school in 1858. They also show him listed in the Collegiate Department as a junior in the 1860–61 class. Sadly, Robert died in 1862.

Chapter 7

A Farm Divided, and a Time of War; President Lincoln's First Inaugural Address

As a young man, Silas stood an erect five feet eleven. He had brown hair and intense gray eyes. The years 1860–1862 were a time of momentous change in his life.

On August 7, 1860, Silas married Maria Aye at Ash Grove. Maria came from Vermillion County, Indiana, to Iroquois County to visit her sister Phebe Aye, who was married to Amos Bishop, one of Mary Ann Bishop's brothers. Maria stayed and became the schoolteacher in Ash Grove.

Maria taught in the public school, and received $50 for three months' work. According to Doris Kogler, a great-granddaughter of Silas's:

> The school treasurer lived in Delrey, so Silas took the teacher to Delrey to draw her salary. It was a long ride both ways and during that ride "Sile" decided he needed a housekeeper and Maria decided he did too and so they were married…both were 18. "Sile" had a new lumber wagon and about 7 o'clock on the evening of their wedding, they got in that wagon and started for Henpeck or Rossville as it is now called. They stopped at the Hoopes' home near the present sight of Hoopeston, went on to Indiana and visited relatives, returning home a week later to take up their home duties on a farm where the groom had been batching. (Cited as *"Cissna Park, Illinois: 1882–1982"* in the bibliography.)

On February 10, 1861, Silas's mother, Mary Ann, married Wesley Harvey. (Some sources say they married in February 1860. I have elected to go with the timing indicated by Beckwith and by the *Watseka Republican*.) Wesley's first wife, Mary Henry, had died in 1859. So, as mentioned earlier, in accordance with Lewis Jr.'s will, his four children became undivided joint owners of the residue of his estate, including the unsold real estate. Mary Ann received just $400. Silas was nineteen; Charles, fifteen; Hannah, twelve; and Sarah, nine.

In 1861, Silas's uncle George Bishop, acting on behalf of Silas, initiated a partition suit in the Iroquois County Circuit Court. He asked the court to divide the remaining Brock family real estate into separate parts for each of the four children. It appears from the case file that a skirmish arose between Mary Ann and her brother George, when she made an effort, unsuccessfully, to assert a right as widow to a certain portion of her husband's real estate (called "dower right"). She made the request notwithstanding the terms of the will and notwithstanding that she had accepted the $400 cash under the will when she remarried.

As a result of the partition suit, the family's 320-acre farm was divided into four separate tracts: for Silas, 85 acres; for Charles, 40 acres; for Hannah, 85 acres; and for Sarah, 99 acres. (The status of the remaining 11 acres is unclear.) The partition suit also allocated to each child a certain number of residential acres near Pitchin: 5 acres apiece for Silas and Sarah, 22 acres for Charles, and 10 acres for Hannah.

War

President Abraham Lincoln delivered his first inaugural address on March 4, 1861.

> I hold, that in contemplation of universal law, and of the Constitution, the Union of these States is perpetual….In *your* hands, my dissatisfied fellow-countrymen, and not in *mine*, is the momentous issue of civil war. The government will not assail you. You can have no conflict without being yourselves the aggressors.

On April 12, the Confederates bombarded Union soldiers at Fort Sumter, South Carolina.

In June 1861, eight Ash Grove men, including seven farmers and one engineer, responded promptly to events by joining the 25th Illinois Volunteer Infantry Regiment, Company F, for three years. Three months later Thomas Cady, a son of John and Ellen Cady, joined Company C of the 12th Illinois Volunteer Infantry Regiment, also for three years. But far and away the biggest response from Ash Grove came in August 1862, following a call by President Lincoln on July 6, 1862, for volunteers, when at least forty-four men were mustered into the 76th Illinois Volunteer Infantry Regiment ("76th Illinois," or "76th," or the "regiment"). That group included Silas Brock, his brother Charles, his cousin Thomas Roberts, and his future brother-in-law John Gilbert.

A significant number of men from Silas's extended family participated in the war, in various Illinois and Indiana regiments and at various times, as follows:

NAME	RELATIONSHIP TO SILAS BROCK	VOLUNTEER INFANTRY REGIMENT/COMPANY	DURATION OF SERVICE
Silas Brock	—	**76th Illinois, Co. E**	**8/62 – 7/65**
Charles Brock	**Brother**	**76th Illinois, Co. E**	**8/62 – 11/62**
George Bishop	**Uncle**	**113th Illinois, Co. D**	**10/62 – 6/65**
Vinal Aye	**Brother-in-law**	**31st Indiana, Co. A**	**9/61 – 12/65**
John Stidham Gilbert	**Future brother-in-law**	**76th Illinois, Co. K**	**8/62 – 7/65**
John L. Roberts	**First cousin**	**117th Indiana, Co. D or H**	**7/63 – 2/64**

Thomas Roberts	**First cousin**	**76th Illinois, Co. K**	**8/62 – 7/65**
Truman Skeels	**First cousin**	**113th Illinois, Co. D**	**10/62 – 8/64**
Winfield Scott Willoughby	**First cousin**	**150th Illinois, Co. D**	**2/65 – 1/66**
Lewis Roberts Shroyer	**First cousin once removed**	**66th Indiana, Co. A**	**8/62 – 6/65**

(See appendix 5, which includes a summary of service of the three relatives in Indiana regiments.)

The following chart lists the relatives of Lewis Roberts who participated in the war. Included are three of the men from the previous chart.

NAME	RELATIONSHIP TO LEWIS ROBERTS	VOLUNTEER INFANTRY REGIMENT/COMPANY	DURATION OF SERVICE
John L. Roberts	**Grandson**	**117th Indiana, Co. D**	**7/63 – 2/64**
Thomas Roberts	**Grandson**	**76th Illinois, Co. K**	**8/62 – 7/65**
Lewis Roberts Shroyer	**Great-Grandson**	**66th Indiana, Co. A**	**8/62 – 6/65**
Elisha Hawkins	**Grandnephew**	**76th Illinois, Co. K (recruit)**	**12/63 – 7/64 (killed in action near Jackson, MS)**
James Wesley Chess	**Grandnephew**	**12th Indiana, Co. A**	**10/61 (recruit) – 5/62**
William Gasaway	**Step-Grandnephew**	**67th Indiana, Co. H**	**8/62 – 2/63 (died of typhoid fever at Young's Point, LA)**

That group included two sons—John and Thomas—and one grandson—Lewis Roberts Shroyer—of Jacob Roberts and Nancy Brock.

John Nunamaker's son, John Wesley Nunamaker, a resident of Bernadotte, Fulton County, Illinois, joined the 84th Illinois Volunteer Infantry Regiment, Company F, at Quincy, Illinois in August 1862.

At least seventy-nine men from Ash Grove enlisted, in various regiments and at various times, including those who joined in 1861, as summarized in the following chart:

REGIMENT/ COMPANY	MUSTERING IN DATE/PLACE	TERM OF ENLISTMENT	NUMBER OF ASH GROVE MEN
25th Ill. Volunteer Infantry, Company F	**August 4, 1861 US Arsenal Park St. Louis, MO**	**3 years**	**8**
12th Ill. Volunteer Infantry, Company C	**September 8, 1861 Paducah, KY**	**3 years**	**1**
76th Ill. Volunteer Infantry, Company E	**August 22, 1862 Kankakee, IL**	**3 years**	**17**
76th Ill. Volunteer Infantry, Company K	**August 22, 1862 – 27 in Kankakee, IL December 1863 – 2 in Danville, IL**	**3 years**	**27**
113th Ill. Volunteer Infantry, Company D ("Third Chicago Board	**October 1, 1862 Camp Hancock Chicago, IL**	**3 years**	**7**

of Trade
Regiment")

Regiment	Date/Place	Term	Number
76th Ill. Volunteer Infantry, Company K	**December 9, 1863 Danville, IL**	**3 years**	**2 (recruits)**
12th Ill. Volunteer Infantry, Company C	**April 11, 1864 Camp Butler Springfield, IL**	**3 years**	**1 (recruit)**
134th Ill. Volunteer Infantry, Company B	**May 31, 1864 Camp Fry Chicago, IL**	**100 days**	**9**
150th Ill. Volunteer Infantry, Company D	**February 14, 1865 Camp Butler Springfield, IL**	**1 year**	**6**
58th Illinois Volunteer Infantry, Company H Consolidated	**March 8, 1865 Camp Butler Springfield, IL**	**1 year**	**1**
		TOTAL	**79**

I say "at least" seventy-nine men from Ash Grove joined, because the listings in the Illinois State Archives include numerous men for whom no residence is indicated. The stated ages of those seventy-nine men ranged from eighteen to forty-five, though how many may have misrepresented their ages is impossible to say. The average stated age was about twenty-five. Only sixteen of those men were born in Iroquois County; thirty-two were born in Indiana, and sixteen in Ohio. At least twenty-eight were married. Only a dozen of them were landowners.

Regarding the Ash Grove men included in the foregoing chart other than those who served in the 76th Illinois, see appendix 6. One of the men who served in the 113th Illinois, Truman Skeels, a cousin of Silas's, was court-martialed in August 1864. That incident is described in chapter 9.

Silas kept a diary of his experiences in the war. However, family history says that, upon his death, that diary was taken apart and several pages given to each of his ten grandchildren. That group included my father; his files did not include any such pages.

Lamentably, I have seen copies of only five pages of the diary, from Bill Borror, a great-grandson of Silas. (Three brief quotations from those pages are included in what follows.) I do not know where the remaining pages are, if they still exist. Nor have I located any wartime letters between Silas and Maria.

Shortly after the Civil War the surviving members of the 76th Illinois met briefly in Watseka, but then did not meet again as a group until October 1886, when the first reunion of the "Society of Survivors of the 76th Regiment Illinois Infantry" was held in Kankakee. Beginning in that year, the regiment held annual reunions. No reunion was held in 1893 because of the World's Columbian Exposition in Chicago. The society created written proceedings for each reunion, at least through 1909. A specific numbered reunion is referred to in what follows as a "Reunion of Survivors."

Chapter 8

Civil War, July 1862–July 1863: 76th Illinois from Kankakee to Vicksburg and Jackson, Mississippi; Emancipation Proclamation

July–August 1862
Calls for Volunteers

On July 6, 1862, President Lincoln called for 300,000 volunteers to enlist in the Union army for three-year terms. On August 5, the government called for an additional 300,000 militia to serve nine-month enlistments. It established quotas by state. The secretary of war threatened to impose a draft on any state that did not meet its quota of three-year enlistments before August 18. Illinois's combined quota under both calls was set at 52,296 volunteers. The state exceeded that quota.

Historians have suggested a number of motivations for that response. One is from Clyde Walton, the Illinois state historian: "In 1862 it was considered something of a disgrace to be drafted, and there is reason to believe that some men enlisted because of the threat of conscription." Another is elaborated in the following excerpt from the 1861–1862 report of Illinois Adj. Gen. Allen Fuller:

The floating population of the State who would enlist had already done so. These new volunteers must come, if come at all, from the farmers and mechanics of the State. Farmers were

in the midst of their harvests, and it is no exaggeration to say, that inspired by a holy zeal, animated by a common purpose, and firmly resolved on rescuing this Government from the very brink of ruin, and restoring it to the condition our fathers left, over fifty thousand of them left their harvests ungathered—their tools on their benches—the plows in the furrows, and turned their backs upon home and loved ones, AND BEFORE ELEVEN DAYS EXPIRED THE DEMANDS OF THE COUNTRY WERE MET, AND BOTH QUOTAS WERE FILLED!!
Six of these new regiments were organized, mustered, armed, and clothed, and sent into the field in August (Eddy 1865, 1: 125-127).

August 1862
Formation of the 76th Illinois

One of the six regiments referred to by Adjutant General Fuller was the 76th Illinois, organized at Kankakee, Illinois, and led by Col. Alonzo Mack, a member of the Illinois State Senate.

The regiment elected Samuel Busey of Urbana, Illinois, as lieutenant colonel. It was mustered and clothed in August, but, contrary to the adjutant general's report, not armed until September at Columbus, Kentucky.

At full strength, a regiment was comprised of 1,025 men—ten companies of 101 men each, plus a regimental staff of 15. A colonel commanded a regiment; a captain commanded a company.

Tens of thousands pitched in! Whatever the motivations, the response to the government's calls for volunteers was extraordinary. Musicians played "We Are Coming, Father Abraham":

We are coming, we are coming
our Union to restore,
We are coming, Father Abraham,
300,000 more.

Silas Brock and Charles Brock

Silas at twenty enlisted for three years on August 8, 1862, and he was mustered in as a private at Kankakee on August 22. He joined Company E of the 76th Illinois under the command of Capt. Abram Irvin, a twenty-eight-year-old minister. Silas received a bounty of $25 and a premium of $2. His pay as a private was $13 per month.

Meanwhile, in Ash Grove, Maria was expecting a child.

Silas was one of seventeen men, all farmers, from Ash Grove who enlisted for three years and who were assigned to Company E. That group included Silas's brother Charles, who was sixteen at enlistment on August 15 but who represented himself as nineteen. Charles was mustered in as a musician. He was discharged for disability—tuberculosis, contracted prior to enlistment—on November 22, 1862, in Jackson, Tennessee.

Thomas Roberts and John Gilbert

Twenty-seven other men from Ash Grove, including twenty-eight farmers and one mechanic, also enlisted for three years in August 1862, and they were assigned to Company K of the 76th Illinois. Silas's first cousin, Thomas Roberts, the fourth son of Jacob Roberts and Nancy Brock, was included in that company. He enlisted at age twenty-nine, and he was mustered in as a sergeant.

Company K included John Gilbert, who enlisted at age nineteen on July 22. He would marry Silas's sister Hannah after the war. The mechanic in the group was Sgt. William Duke, born in Manchester, England. Joseph Davis, a thirty-eight-year-old Ash Grove farmer, became the captain of Company K.

Brothers in the War

Silas and Charles were not the only example of brothers from Ash Grove enlisting in the war.

The Spain brothers were children of William and Mary Cole Spain of Champaign County, Ohio. Four of the brothers—James, Hamilton, Moses, and Elijah—moved from Ohio to Ash Grove. James, Hamilton, and Moses joined the 76th Illinois, Company E, with Silas, for three years. Elijah became a member of the 150th Illinois, Company D, in February 1865, for one year. Two other brothers, John and Philander, did not move to Ash Grove but also served in the Union army, in Ohio regiments. Six brothers from one family! Extraordinary, but I assume not unique.

The regimental band played "The Battle Cry of Freedom":

Yes we'll rally round the flag, boys, we'll rally once again,
Shouting the battle cry of freedom,
We will rally from the hillside, we'll gather from the plain,
Shouting the battle cry of freedom.

September–December 1862
In the Western Theater of the War

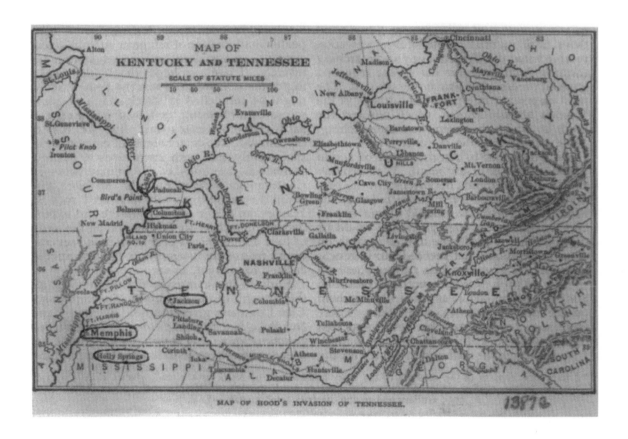

Map showing the locations of Cairo, Illinois; Columbus, Kentucky; Jackson, Tennessee;
Memphis, Tennessee; and Holly Springs, Mississippi (circled by author in red)

(Cited as *"Map of Kentucky and Tennessee"* in the bibliography)

Promptly after mustering in, the 76th Illinois moved from Kankakee by rail (the Illinois Central Railroad, which ran through Iroquois County) on open flat cars to Cairo, Illinois, and from there by boat to Columbus, Kentucky. There the soldiers were armed with British Enfield rifle muskets captured from the Confederate steamer *Fair Play.* They also received their canteens, knapsacks, and haversacks.

ALBERT P. CUNNINGHAM.
2nd Lieut. Co. G.

2nd Lt. Albert Cunningham
Champaign, Illinois
(3rd Reunion of Survivors 48
[1888])

Many years after the war, 2nd Lt. Albert Cunningham of the 76th, Company G, had this to say about the Enfields:

> Our regiment as you all remember, landed on the dark and bloody ground

about the last of August, 1862, at Columbus, Kentucky, 25 miles south of Cairo, without a gun or a musket to defend ourselves with and make the enemy wish they had staid at home. We had not long to wait, however, for soon we were fully armed with that very useless weapon the Enfield rifle. They surely were very harmless to the man at the other end. But I suppose they were the best that our "Uncle Samuel," could give us at that time, and it is now too late to complain (6th Reunion of Survivors 8-9 [1891]).

One source says that, in March 1864, the regiment acquired Springfield rifle muskets to replace the Enfields.

The daily routine at Columbus began with reveille at four thirty a.m., fall in for roll call and for the "sogering" of drills and dress parades, inspections, sentry duty, etc.; then tattoo and roll call at nine in the evening. The soldiers learned fatigue and picket duty. In the words of one 76th member, this was the start of learning "soldier sense."

Meanwhile, in the Eastern Theater of the war, the Battle of Antietam in Maryland took place on September 17. The carnage on both sides was terrible. That day turned out to be the bloodiest single day of the conflict—almost twenty-three thousand killed, wounded, and captured/missing.

Back home, Maria buried their infant son in Pitchin Cemetery. I have not identified a tombstone marking his grave.

On September 21,

Silas's first born son,

just nine days old,

died in Maria's arms.

Their Ash Grove farm

seemed suddenly cold.

The wind blew dust

across the fields, swirling,

the fence gate swinging,

the corn rows rustling.

"May you rest in peace, my son,

and may this war end soon."

Charles M. Brock

On October 4, the 76th struck tents in Columbus and moved south by freight train to Jackson, Tennessee, and then farther south again to Bolivar, Tennessee. On October 5, Pvt. Oliver Nail of the 76th Illinois, Company K, died at Columbus from the effects of a kick by a horse.

The 76th camped near Bolivar, where a measles epidemic broke out, until early November, when the regiment marched with full knapsacks roughly twenty-five miles south to La Grange, Tennessee. It remained in La Grange until November 28.

Pvt. Aaron Russell, Pvt. George Thomas, and Pvt. Jonathan Clawson, all of Company K, died of disease at La Grange—Russell (measles) on November 16, Thomas (measles) on December 2, and Clawson (pneumonia) on December 4. Pvt. Hamilton Spain of Company E died of disease (pneumonia)

at a field hospital in La Grange on December 17.

Pvt. John Gilbert (Silas's future brother-in-law) of Company K was in the hospital in La Grange during November and December.

Following is an entry from Silas's diary from November 24 when the regiment was camped in La Grange:

Ordered to march at 6 O'clock

Called on to fall in line at

the time. Fell in   stood in

ranks awhile and

then fell out   and ready

to march at any moment

Marched at 12 O'clock.

Hurry up and wait!

Major General Grant's Central Mississippi Campaign
November 1862–January 1863

In November, Maj. Gen. Ulysses S. Grant initiated his campaign along the Mississippi Central Railroad, including the 76th Illinois coming from La Grange, with the capture of Vicksburg as the ultimate objective.

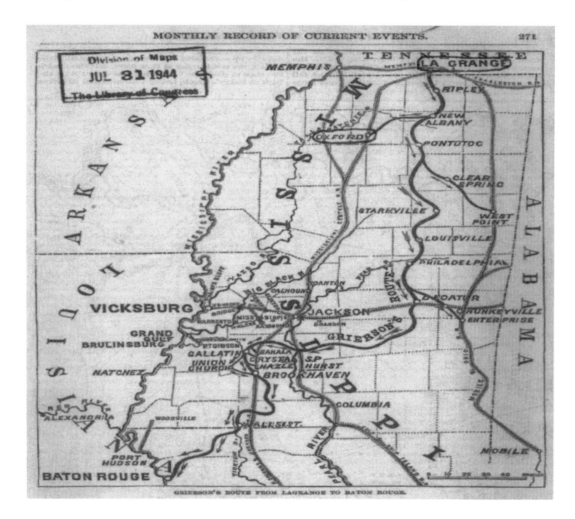

Map showing the locations of La Grange, Tennessee; and Oxford, Mississippi
(circled by author in red)

(Cited as *"Grierson's route from La Grange to Baton Rouge"*
in the bibliography)

We entered Holly Springs about ten o'clock one night,
Singing patriotic songs and aching for a fight.
Next day we drove the enemy in haste past Lumkin's Mill,
And we camped there a few days in the storm up on Soap Hill.
Then crossed the Tallehatchie, passed the village of Abbyville
With the rebels in full retreat, a little ahead of us still.
Then on to Oxford next and camped a while in the woods
Near Springdale, where we waited for the arrival of our goods.

76th Illinois QM Sgt. John Shuck wrote those lines, as quoted in the proceedings of the 1st Reunion of Survivors 11 (1886). Holly Springs is located on the previous map.

Quartermaster Sergeant John Shuck
Urbana, Illinois
(3rd Reunion of Survivors 14 [1888])

Pvt. Hiram Harris of Company K died of disease at Oxford on December 17.

On December 22, the Federals learned that Confederate Maj. Gen. Earl Van Dorn captured the Union advance supply base at Holly Springs.

Consequently, the Union soldiers were forced to reverse course and return to northern Mississippi. The regiment's food supply was drastically short, forcing the soldiers to live almost entirely on cornmeal for several weeks.

Silas's diary entry for December 25:

Dec 25   Christmas
morning got up and got
breakfast   stood around
til   time for dinner   got
dinner   marching order
at 2 P.M.   marched two
miles   and camped.

On January 1, 1863, President Lincoln issued the Emancipation Proclamation.

On January 5, the 76th arrived
back in Holly Springs, which the
Confederates had abandoned. Silas
wrote the following entries in his diary
for the fifth through the tenth:

Marching orders to march

the 5th at 7 O'clock

5th All ready and started at

the time   we marched to

Holly Springs   got there

a little before sun down

making a march of about

12 miles and camped   it

rained some through

the night.

6th Some of the teams

ordered out—foraging

nothing else going on

in camp.

Wednesday 7th

Guard detailed at 6 O'clock…

to guard a train of teams

went to headquarters to

report   stacked arms and

Waited for the teams

awhile   formed   took arms

and came to camp   no more

for today   except dress

parade   Thursday 8th

Guards detailed to guard the

108 had to stand   3 hours

all for this day

Friday 9th   Relieved from

guard this morning

and come into camp got ready

and went to town   some

buildings burnt in town

last night   Come back from

and wrote part of a

letter home

Saturday 10th   There has

been a fire in town most all

night.

Back to Tennessee
January–May 1863

The regiment arrived in Moscow, Tennessee, on January 11, finally on full rations. There the soldiers learned that Col. Mack ("little Mack") had resigned to return to the Illinois State Senate.   Lt. Col. Samuel Busey was promoted to colonel.

Surgeon Franklin Blades
Middleport, Illinois (later Watseka)
(Beckwith)

Regimental surgeon Franklin Blades wrote a letter from Moscow on January 20 directly to Maj. Gen. Grant, requesting leave because of a dangerously sick child at home:

Sir: I crave your indulgence for addressing you personally. Extreme anxiety has induced me to make this apparently desperate effort to get leave of absence for a short time— say fifteen days—as I should not forgive myself were I not to make the effort however faint the prospect of success.

 I have late intelligence that my little son—an only child—is lying very low and not expected to live. My wife sends to me imploringly to come home if possible. Of course, I cannot do so without your permission.

 I am surgeon of the 76th Reg. Ill. Vol. Infy. in the 4th Div. The Reg. will not suffer by my absence, as there are two efficient assistant surgeons now on duty with the Regiment.

 Trusting that the circumstances will appeal to your sympathy in making this unusual application.

Col. Samuel Busey
Urbana, Illinois
(2nd Reunion of Survivors 1 [1887])

Capt. Irvin of Company E was sick in the hospital at La Grange.

Col. Busey and Maj. Gen. Grant approved the request. I assume surgeon Blades felt empowered to write directly to the general, because he was personally acquainted with President Lincoln (see chapter 10).

February–May 1863
From Moscow to Memphis

On February 5, the 76th marched in a column of twos about ten miles from Moscow to Lafayette.

Pvt. (later Sgt. Maj.) Sylvanus Cass Munhall
Watseka, Illinois
(2nd Reunion of Survivors 24 [1887])

The following is from a letter dated February 9 from Pvt. Sylvanus Cass Munhall (nicknamed "Urchin") of Company B, a war correspondent, to his newspaper regarding that march to Lafayette:

> On the 5th inst. our regiment marched from Moscow, Tennessee, to this place, over roads that would have been considered impassable in time of peace; the snow was about four inches deep, and the depth of the mud under the snow was without limitation….The northeast wind blew cold, and the snow fell thick and fast….[We] camped about 3 o'clock P.M. in the muddiest place we could find near the village of La Fayette….After we were halted and arms stacked, we commenced work shoveling snow and mud, hoping to discover dry soil enough on which to pitch our tents, but our hopes were blasted and our efforts defeated. To sleep on the frozen ground without fire, or in the mud with fire, seemed to be our destiny. Choosing the latter we pitched our tents, built our fire in the center (Sibley tents), took our little ration of "hard tack" and "sow belly," and wilted down with three rails under us crossways to keep us above board….The night proved a severe one, but morning found us above the surface….The mud is rapidly drying up, the average depth is now about sixteen inches. We hope to leave here for Memphis soon as we are now well fixed. It spoils soldiers to remain in good quarters long (Beckwith 1880, I: 287-288).

On March 9 or 10, the 76th undertook a three-day march to Memphis, where it set up camp in an apple orchard.

On February 21, Pvt. Isaac VanHorn of Company K died of disease (catarrh) at Memphis. On March 18, Pvt. Benjamin Bratton of Company E died of disease (febris typhoid) at La Grange. Pvt. Joel Vaughn of Company K died of disease (chronic diarrhea) on April 11 at St. Louis.

May–July 4, 1863
Siege of Vicksburg

On the following page is a map showing the locations of Millikens Bend, Louisiana; Young's Point, Louisiana; Grand Gulf, Mississippi; Yazoo River, Mississippi; Chickasaw Bayou, Mississippi; and Vicksburg, Mississippi. Locations are circled in red by the author. This map is cited as "Tomlinson, George W." in the bibliography.

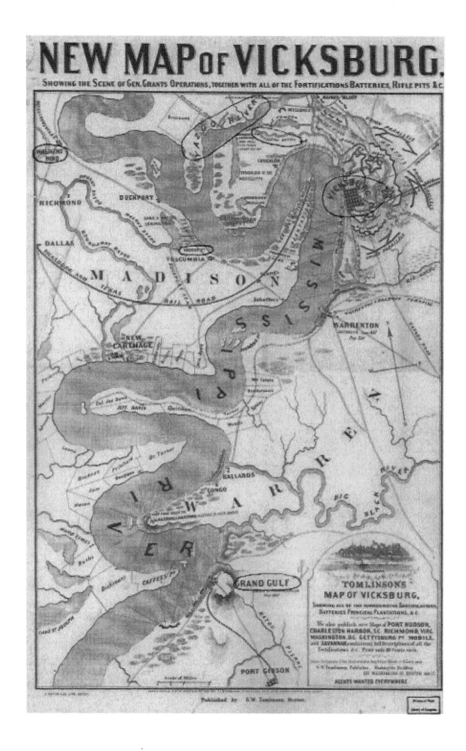

In May, the 76th Illinois set off with other soldiers

on a fleet of steamers…down the Mississippi River. The steamer "Fort Wayne," carrying the Seventy-sixth, was fired into in the night by a band of Guerrillas from the Arkansas shore. Two men were wounded and the boat disabled. The Regiment landed in the morning and burned the buildings on the plantations in the vicinity. The disabled boat was towed down the river with the fleet to Young's Point, Louisiana, where it landed May 17th.

On the 18th the Regiment marched across the Point to the river below Vicksburg and embarked for Grand Gulf, and returned to Young's Point on the 20th and immediately embarked for "Chicasaw Bayou" on the Yazoo River, at which place it debarked on the same day; was engaged in closing up the lines in the rear of Vicksburg until after the charge, when it was placed on the left of the besieging lines, and bravely held its place close under the Rebel guns until the final surrender [of the Confederate forces in Vicksburg] July 4th.

(Cited as "Illinois Secretary of State, Illinois State Archives: Illinois Adjutant General's Report: Regimental and Unit Histories" in the bibliography.)

Brig. Gen. Jacob Lauman's forces, including the 76th Illinois, were "placed on the left of the besieging lines," south of the city, about May 25.

First Lt. Peter Williams of Company E, preacher of the Methodist Episcopal Church in Milford, Illinois, was shot while on picket duty and died during the "investment" (siege) of Vicksburg, on June 21. (See chapter 11.)

No Ash Grove men were killed or wounded during the siege.

Maj. George Harrington
Watseka, Illinois
(2nd Reunion of Survivors 16 [1887])

While at the regimental hospital near Vicksburg in June, Maj. George Harrington of the 76th resigned because of disability, suffering from chronic dysentery. Surgeon Franklin Blades certified the major's condition:

[O]n account of disability from the same disease, he has not been on duty over three months during the period of nearly ten months [since mustering in]. He is entirely unfit to perform any duty at this time and in my opinion his health is so permanently broken down that he cannot again be able to discharge the duties of his office. I am of the opinion that he will die should he be obliged to remain in the Service.

Sgt. Thomas Roberts of Company K, Silas's first cousin, was sick from June 9 and admitted to the hospital in St. Louis on August 28 with chronic diarrhea. He returned to duty on October 13.

In the Eastern Theater, the Battle of Gettysburg took place on July 1-3. Both armies suffered enormous casualties. I have seen various estimates, some in the neighborhood of fifty thousand killed, wounded, and captured/missing.

July 1863
Siege of Jackson, Mississippi

After the surrender of Vicksburg on July 4, the 76th moved with Maj. Gen. William Tecumseh Sherman against Jackson, Mississippi, about forty miles' straight-line distance from Vicksburg. Skirmishes with the Confederates took place en route at Big Black River and Champion Hill.   Maj. Gen. Sherman's army laid siege to Jackson and finally occupied the town on July 17. Then the regiment returned to Vicksburg, after seeing the town of Jackson half-burned.

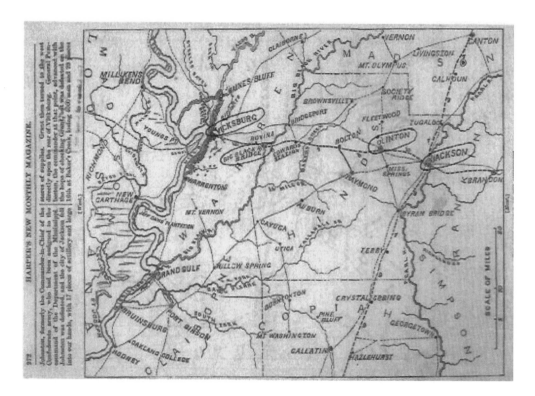

Map showing the locations of Vicksburg, Mississippi; Jackson, Mississippi; Big Black River Bridge, Mississippi; and Clinton, Mississippi (circled by author in red)

(Cited as *"The Seat of War on the Mississippi"* in the bibliography)

Chapter 9

Civil War, August 1863–August 1864: 76th Illinois in Mississippi and Louisiana; President Lincoln at Gettysburg; Battle of the Crossroads; General Court-Martial in the 113th Illinois

August 1863–June 1864 76th From Natchez to Meridian to Yazoo City

Silas took a thirty-day furlough beginning August 5, returning to Ash Grove for the first time after a full year away.

Col. Busey was detached on recruiting service in Springfield, Illinois, in August and September. On October 10, he was detailed on a general court-martial.

From August until November 28, the 76th was on duty in Natchez, Mississippi. In September, it made an expedition with Brig. Gen. Marcellus Crocker to Louisiana, after which soldiers renamed the 76th "the Alligator Regiment."

In November, President Lincoln consecrated the cemetery in Gettysburg.

President Lincoln traveled
by train to Gettysburg
to consecrate the cemetery.

The committee invited Lincoln:
"It is the desire that,
after the oration, you,
as chief executive of the nation,
formally set apart
these grounds to their sacred use
by a few appropriate remarks."

Of the oration,
Everett's two-hour description—
now all but forgotten—
of three days that left eight thousand
dead:
"He talked like a historian,"
one paper said. "He gave us
plenty of words but no heart."

The president's consecration
of the cemetery
became our dedication
and lives on in memory.

Charles M. Brock

Pvt. James Higginson of Company E died of disease (chronic diarrhea) at Natchez on November 23.

In late 1863, the 76th camped near Vicksburg at Camp Cowan.

In February, the 76th participated in Maj. Gen. Sherman's Meridian campaign in east-central Mississippi near the Alabama border.

General Grant ordered the army of the Tennessee to keep open the Mississippi River, and maintain our control of its east bank...."To destroy the enemy's means of approaching the River with artillery and trains...[Gen. Sherman] determined to organize a large column of infantry and move with it to Meridian, effectually breaking up the Southern Mississippi Railway, while a cavalry force should move from Memphis to meet him, and perform the same work with respect to the Mobile & Ohio Railway."

The cavalry did not show up as ordered.

On the 16th [of February] the railways centering there were "inspected." Says Colonel Bowman: "The depots, storehouses, arsenals, offices, hospitals, hotels and cantonments in the town were burned, and during the next five days, with axes, sledges, crowbars, clambers and fire, [Maj. Gen.Stephen] Hurlbut's corps destroyed on the north and east sixty miles of ties and iron, one locomotive and eight bridges; and [Maj. Gen. James] McPherson's corps, on the south and west, fifty-five miles of railway, fifty-three bridges, 6,075 feet of trestle work, nineteen locomotives, twenty-eight steam cars" (Eddy 1865, II 160, 162).

In early March, the 76th returned to camp near Vicksburg at Camp Hebron, doing picket and camp duty.

In April, regimental surgeon Franklin Blades resigned for disability. He had been afflicted with chronic dysentery since July 1863 at Jackson, Mississippi. One examining doctor in Middleport, Illinois (later Watseka), said that he "strongly suspected ulceration in the large intestine." That doctor recommended a "bracing vigorous anti-billious climate" outside the South. "[H]e would be at great hazard to life were he to undertake to join his regiment in Mississippi and undertake to do duty in his present condition."

In early May, the regiment joined the command of Brig. Gen. John McArthur on his expedition to Yazoo City, Mississippi, participating in a skirmish at the town of Benton.

Through Yazoo Valley we marched, and found the enemy in force.
At Benton, with artillery, musketry and horse,
We valiantly then fought them, for three long days, or more,
And drove them all *pell mell*....

QM Sgt. John Shuck (1st Reunion of Survivors 14 [1886])

They occupied Yazoo City, followed by a return to Vicksburg.

On June 13, Ash Grove farmer Sgt. Maj. Joseph Schooley, who had been promoted to sergeant major from private in June 1863, was discharged from the 76th Illinois in order to accept appointment as captain of the 66th Regiment, United States Colored Infantry. That regiment was organized on March 11, 1864, from the Mississippi Volunteers 4th Regiment Infantry (African descent), which had been organized at Vicksburg on December 11, 1863.   The 66th did post and garrison duty at various locations, saw action in several places, and was mustered out on March 20, 1866. (Cited as "United States National Park Service. The Civil War--Battle Unit Details" in the bibliography.)

July 1864
Battle of the Crossroads
near Jackson, Mississippi

In July, the 76th participated in an expedition under the command of Maj. Gen. Henry Slocum, to Jackson, Mississippi. On the return from Jackson to Vicksburg, intense battles occurred on July 6 and 7 between Jackson and Clinton, a small town on the Vicksburg & Jackson Railroad.   See the map cited as "The Seat of War on the Mississippi" in chapter 8 for the locations of Jackson and Clinton.

A letter published in the *Chicago Tribune* of July 21, 1864, described that battle. (3rd Reunion of Survivors 45-52 [1888]). The engagement took place during the late afternoon of July 6 and morning of July 7, at a point some three miles west of Jackson, known as "Crossroads," where the Canton road intersected the main Jackson road. In that engagement, the Confederates had some 3,500 cavalry and infantry, while the Union forces did not exceed 2,000 men.

The Union army left Jackson about 4:00 p.m. on July 6. They proceeded only a short distance, with the 76th in the advance, when they were halted.

Artillery was now put in position, cavalry thrown out as skirmishers, and the lines established by the infantry—everything in position, and the ball opened. Heavy firing from both sides was kept up until the shades of darkness set in, when both armies retired, our men taking position and lying on their arms until the coming morn, when long ere the sun ascended from behind the hills of the far distant east, the skirmishing commenced.

The letter to the *Tribune* continued with a description of the action on the morning of July 7:

Heavy firing, both from artillery and musketry was kept up continually until seven o'clock, neither party seeming to gain any advantage, until finally the 2d Brigade, of the gallant old 4th Division, were ordered to advance, the 76th Illinois Infantry in front as skirmishers, and the 46th Illinois Infantry, as a support. And advance they did, until the entire line was within some twenty-five yards of the enemy, who lay in one position, which they had established the previous evening, under cover, lying in the edge of a body of heavy timber, while on the contrary our lines were exposed to their whole fire, being in an open field which inclined towards them. In this position these two regiments lay for five hours until the entire [Union supply] train had passed, without the loss of a wagon, and it has been asserted that this command saved all from destruction, by their gallantry and desperate fighting. Too much credit and praise cannot be attributed to the officers and men—no braver ever entered the field of battle. Strange as it may seem, the 76th did not lose an officer, and had twenty-one on the field, but lost about one hundred men out of three hundred and seventy-five. Lieut. Col. C. C. Jones had his horse shot four times while riding along the lines, the last shot proving fatal, but he never retired from the field, although his leg was fractured by his falling off the horse.

Lt. Col. C. C. Jones
Morris, Illinois
(2nd Reunion of
Survivors 8 [1887])

After five hours hard fighting, orders came to fall back, and it was with the greatest difficulty that this regiment escaped capture, as they were compelled to leave all the dead and seriously wounded on the field, being obliged to crawl some two hundred yards under a heavy and galling fire of musketry and artillery, after which they reformed the line and crossed a large opening some two miles in width, under a constant fire of grape, canister and musketry, when we rejoined our command in good order,

receiving the compliments of the General [Brig. Gen. E. S. Dennis] and his staff, who had given us up as lost, for fighting our way out.

"Grape" is short for "grapeshot", a number of small iron balls fired together from a cannon. "Canister" is small bullets packed in cases that fit the bore of an artillery piece or gun.

The *Tribune's* letter included a list of casualties suffered by the 76th Illinois. Silas received a "slight" wound on his right leg.

Pvt. Elijah Bratten, Pvt. Samuel Rowley, and Pvt. Elisha Hawkins, all of Company K, were killed in action on July 7. Elisha Hawkins was a recruit who joined the 76th in December 1863, sixteen months after the regiment had been organized. He was a grandnephew of Lewis Roberts (see chapter 7).

Pvt. Samuel Montgomery of Company E died on July 11 of wounds to both hips suffered in action on July 7. Pvt. Joseph McKinley of Company E died at Ash Grove on March 20, 1865, of severe wounds suffered in action on the road between Jackson and Clinton.

The 76th returned to Vicksburg on July 9. On July 23, prisoners captured at Jackson were exchanged, and they rejoined their regiments.

The regiment's musicians played "Tenting on the Old Camp Ground":

Many are the hearts that are weary tonight,
Wishing for the war to cease;
Many are the hearts looking for the right
To see the dawn of peace.
Tenting tonight, tenting tonight,
Tenting on the old campground.

On July 29, the 76th moved to Morganzia, Louisiana, on the marine boat *B. J. Adams*.

August 1864
General Court-Martial in the 113th Illinois

In August, two soldiers of the 113th Illinois, Company D—Pvt. Michael Lovett from Onarga, Illinois, and Pvt. Truman Skeels, Silas's cousin from Ash Grove—were court-martialed for allegedly helping a prisoner escape from the notorious Irving Block Military Prison in Memphis.

Before addressing the court-martial, a look at Skeels's full service record is in order. He was sick when he was mustered in on October 1, 1862, and he spent October and November in Ash Grove. On November 26, he was transferred sick to St. Louis, where he remained through June 1863. His service record does not indicate the nature of his illness. He was in Corinth, Mississippi during July and August, but detached from his company. He finally joined Company D on September 12, almost a year after being mustered in.

As to the court-martial, both Lovett and Skeels were with a

detachment of Company D as guards at the Irving Block Prison, beginning in May 1864. That detachment also included Pvt. William Wilson, according to the court-martial record. More about him shortly.

Lt. Col. John Marsh, 24th Regiment Veteran Reserve Corps, had inspected the prison and issued a report in April 1864. US Judge Adv. Gen. Joseph Holt relayed the information in that report in a letter to President Lincoln dated June 24, 1864:

> [T]he prison which is used for the detention of citizens, prisoners of war on their way to the North, and the United States soldiers awaiting trial and which is located in a large block of stores is represented as the filthiest place the inspector ever saw occupied by human beings. The whole management and government of the prisoners could not be worse! Discipline and order are unknown. Food sufficient but badly served. In a dark wet cellar I found twenty-eight prisoners chained to a wet floor, where they had been constantly confined, many of them for several months, one since November 16, 1863, and are not for a moment released, even to relieve the calls of nature. With a single exception these men have had no trial. (Cited as "Historic Memphis—Irving Block Prison" in the bibliography.)

The prison commandant at the time of Lt. Col. Marsh's report was Capt. George Williams, who was also provost marshal (head of the military police in Memphis). He was replaced on May 26 as commandant by Capt. Henry Hoyt, who was detached from the 113th Illinois, Company A. It appears that

Capt. Williams remained as provost marshal.

The prisoner who escaped on the night of July 22, one James C. Snow, was confined on a charge of murder. No doubt, the escape was embarrassing to Capt. Hoyt, especially given the history of the prison. No doubt he was anxious to avoid the criticism of mismanagement directed at his predecessor.

During the trial, the prosecution called three witnesses against Skeels:

(1) **Sgt. Asher Kiley, who, according to the court-martial record, was a member of the 114th Illinois Volunteers, and a clerk at the prison.** Kiley said that Skeels was confined in irons in the cellar of the prison together with the escaped prisoner's father, James H. Snow. Kiley hid behind some barrels in the cellar, at the commandant's direction, for three or four hours to listen to the conversation between Skeels and the father. The father said during that conversation that he had given Pvt. Lovett $100 to give to his son, and that he had taken a receipt for the money, which he kept in a trunk in his room in a house in Memphis. On the basis of that conversation Capt. Hoyt found the receipt, and the father was arrested, because the receipt, signed by Lovett, stated that the money was "received from J. C. Snow in Part Pay for Survisis Rendered him in his escape from Prison." During the conversation in the cellar, Skeels said he knew nothing about the payment or the receipt. The

father was tried for bribery before a military commission two weeks before this court-martial. I don't know what his sentence was. He made an unexplained comment during the conversation with Skeels to the effect that he and the provost marshal "belonged to an 'order' that would not allow him to be kept long."

(2) **Pvt. William Wilson, who was on guard duty with Lovett and Skeels on the night of July 22, according to the court-martial record.** Wilson said that, between midnight and 2:00 a.m. on the twenty-second, he was stationed inside the prison wall, and outside the iron grates that enclosed the son's cell. He asserted that Skeels was on duty as a sentinel at the outer gate of the main prison. He added that he saw someone on the steps of the prison but he wasn't certain that it was the prisoner who escaped. Wilson said that, about four days after the escape, he told the commandant that Skeels had asked him to cooperate in the escape and had offered him money. But he claimed that he did not receive any money and he didn't know if Skeels received any money. Wilson was not punished and he was transferred from the 113th to the 120th Illinois Volunteers.

(3) **Capt. Hoyt, the commandant.** Hoyt said that he often observed Skeels "carrying provisions to the prisoners from the Restaurant outside." Hoyt said

he put a stop to that practice. He asserted that he saw Skeels on duty at the front gate at midnight, but he did not know what time the prisoner escaped.

Skeels pleaded not guilty. He had no attorney, and he did not present a defense. Nor did he appeal the decision. Both Lovett and Skeels were found guilty. They were transferred to the prison in Alton, Illinois, at hard labor for the duration of the war. They were sentenced to wear a ball and chain attached to their legs "each alternate week," to forfeit all pay, and to be dishonorably discharged. The Alton military prison has been described as pestilential and rat-infested.

The receipt, apparently signed by Lovett, was clearly damning in his case. But Skeels's guilt turned on the testimony of Pvt. Wilson. Was the latter telling the truth, or did he concoct the story in order to protect himself or to curry favor? He started to explain his motivation at the trial, but he was cut off in mid-statement.

I have found no record of a Sgt. Asher Kiley from the 114th Illinois, either in the Illinois State Archives or in the National Archives. I assume that is not definitive. However, it strikes me as curious, given the large number of service records that I was able to locate (listed in the bibliography). Who was the individual sent to the basement to spy on Skeels and Snow?

As to Pvt. Wilson, his service record states that, during July and August 1864, he was on "daily duty Twin Bridges Memphis & C.R.R." It says nothing about duty at the Irving Block Military Prison. So that raises another question: Was he in fact at the prison when the prisoner escaped? By contrast, Skeels's and Lovett's service records clearly state that, beginning in May 1864, they had "daily duty Irvin [*sic*] Prison."

In short, the record raises more questions than it answers. My own reading of the record, such as it is, is that Skeels was a naïve, well-meaning scapegoat.

One footnote: Capt. Hoyt returned to his regiment in late September or early October. He was captured by Confederate soldiers on October 11 at Eastport, Mississippi; and he remained a prisoner of war, until February 22, 1865, when he was paroled at Messenger's Ferry, Mississippi. I wonder if he was required to wear a ball and chain attached to his legs.

Chapter 10

Civil War, September 1864–August 1865: 76th Illinois from the White River to Fort Barrancas; President Lincoln's Second Inaugural Address; General Lee's Surrender; Battle of Fort Blakely; Assassination; 76th Illinois from Mobile to Galveston to Chicago; Thirteenth Amendment

September 1864–December 1864
From the White River to Memphis

In early September, the regiment boarded the steamer *Nebraska*, and traveled the Mississippi River to the mouth of the White River in Arkansas, camping in the cotton.

> We laid there in camp and fought mosquitos and flies,
> And gnats, and graybacks of an unusual size
> And tried to break the monotony in various ways
> Of quiet camp life during these quiet autumn days.
> At this point a story, I am tempted to relate,
> Its truth is well known, soldiers don't prevaricate.
> When loafing in camp with but little to do,
> The soldiers, in order to keep from getting blue,
> Played games of all kinds; some played seven up,
> And some kept a bank, they called it *chuck-a-luck*.
> Some played chess and cribbage or *fifteen-two*.

QM Sgt. John Shuck
(1st Reunion of Survivors 14 [1886])

Chaplain John W. Monser of the 76th wrote his monthly report for September to Adj. Warren Hickox from the mouth of the White River. The original regimental chaplain, John W. Flower, a Methodist, joined in August 1862, but he resigned in December 1862. The 76th had no chaplain until April 1864, when Monser, a minister born in London, England, and a resident of Urbana, was promoted from private in Company B to chaplain. He was a member of the Disciples of Christ.

Dear Sir:

I take pleasure in furnishing you the following report of the Regiment for the past month. Although we have located in a somewhat monotonous Camp, precluded in many measures, conducive to the soldier's interest, the result obtained has been excellent. HE, ever sagacious, regarding self, yet, prone to the last, to expect succor and comfort to be brought to his tent-door—seeing the isolation and contiguous deprivations of his Camp, forbid this, breaks off his lethargy, and with the prospect of a woody wilderness before him, starts forth on his comfort-hunting excursion, and with flesh and fruit, brings in long lost health! Such has been the good fortune of many recently. There have been fewer men in tent and camp each day, for the past twenty, than has been observed for months, and, as a consequence, emaciated frames are becoming robust bodies, flaccid muscles are transforming to irony sinews. Much of this is also undoubtedly owing to the opportune change of season, and the disposition of war, by which we were suddenly removed to a latitude, more northerly by at least from four to five degrees. But in all, and over all, we mark a high and a kind hand that leads us safely through the sultry glebe; fosters us with parental solicitude and will finally give to us the victory.

I am happy to state we have less really sick men, by half, than we had when I gave in my last report. And with a return of physical health comes a mental and moral invigoration. Many a man, whose animal nature predominates and who heretofore has been in thorough health, has by a

reduction of that nature, through sickness, been brought to a sense of the fact that he has a mind which he has hitherto grossly neglected to cultivate, and while thus prostrated, thus shut off from his former habits of amusement, has picked up courage to explore the region of thought and the world of books. A taste is created for acquiring other men's thoughts—he finds an interchange of ideas an object of deep interest and vast moment. That man is, mentally speaking, redeemed! Many a man, too sorely diseased, is led to reflect on his past history, a history of jealousies and irascible actions, of filchings from men's rights; of cursings and other special irreverences toward God, and timely concludes that instant reformation will be equally productive of happiness below and above.

And, taking a more general view, many a man who rarely if ever lifted a pen to inscribe an idea has been confronted by the dire necessity of closing lines of communication with home, and in the exigency if [sic] the case has manfully buckled on the writing armor and thus secured one of his closest interests and perhaps, closest attachment.

These foregoing remarks are some of the results of my observations in the Regiment. Such cases as have been here used to illustrate, are by no means uncommon among us—and the tendency is in the ultimate for good. As to the general sentiment concerning the success of our arms, so far as I have remarked, 'tis worthy. Men are hopeful "of the coming morrow." —They realize the utility of the precept "Act, Act in the living present."—They are not to be ensnared or shaken in the discharge of their duty to their nation by the siren voice of a whitewashed traitor. They know but one action and this is strike, "till the last armed foe" either retires or "expires." All we need as a Regiment, and indeed as an Army, is to have the fear of God seated within us as a prompting power, and then what might or could withstand us? With that, such Regiment, such Armies, would be, everywhere invincible.

Respectfully Submitted.
John W. Monser
Chaplain

In September and October, Pvt. John Gilbert (Silas's future brother-in-law) was on detached service to the Division Ambulance Corps at the mouth of the White River. In November and December, he was detached to the Ambulance Corps of the 2nd Brigade Reserve Corps.

On November 7, the regiment traveled up the White River to Duvall's Bluff, Arkansas, where the men constructed log cabins for winter quarters and hunted for chickens and deer. Silas went on detail up the Arkansas River. However, the 76th did not stay the winter at Duvall's Bluff. It moved to Memphis by boat for the month of December, at the end of which it was transported on the steamer *Niagara* to New Orleans.

Captain Abram Irvin of the 76th, Company E, was honorably discharged for disability in December. The examining physician stated that he was suffering from bilious intermittent fever, inflammation of the liver, and general debility. First Lt. Cornelius Hogle of Beaver, Illinois was promoted to captain of Company E in March.

One footnote to this period: According to Brock family history, Silas participated in Maj. Gen. Sherman's "March to the Sea," which occurred in November–December 1864. That clearly is incorrect. Silas was with the 76th Illinois in Arkansas at that time.

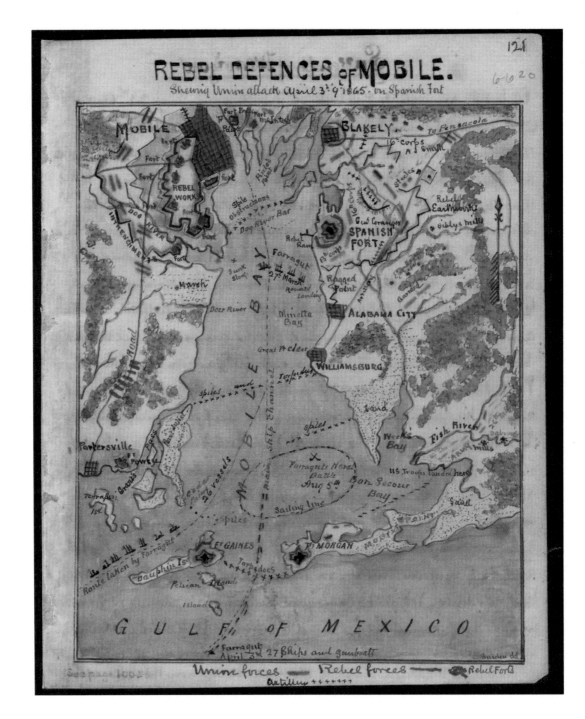

Map showing the locations of Mobile, Alabama; Fort Morgan; Spanish Fort; and Fort Blakely

Map courtesy Virginia Historical Society

(Cited as "Sneden, Robert Knox" in the bibliography)

January–February 1865
From Louisiana to Florida; Tied to a Tree

Until mid-February 1865, the regiment camped at Kenner, north of New Orleans, where, according to the Illinois adjutant general's report, the mud was almost "fathomless." Then the regiment was divided onto three Gulf steamers, the intended destination being Mobile Point, Alabama (Fort Morgan). (See the map on the preceding page for the location of Fort Morgan.) The headquarters personnel and four companies—C, D, Silas's Company E, and I—boarded the *George Peabody* with parts of other regiments and a large number of horses, mules, and wagons (1st Reunion of Survivors 15–16 [1886]). On the night of February 13, they encountered a fierce storm, and they were forced to jettison the animals and wagons in order to save the boat and the men. Finally, they were able to return to New Orleans. Then they crossed Lake Pontchartrain, and they were transported to Fort Morgan and then to Fort Barrancas, near Pensacola, Florida, where they rejoined the other members of the regiment.

According to Colonel Busey's service record, in February at Barrancas a complaint was submitted to the adjutant general's office regarding Col. Busey's endeavoring to transfer musician Isaac Courtwright to another Illinois regiment in exchange for a musician from the latter. It appeared that Col. Busey reduced Courtwright to the ranks from his prior status as principal musician in January, allegedly without assigning any reason for doing so. Courtwright then requested a transfer to a Missouri regiment, which request was denied. Courtwright refused to comply with the order of transfer to the other Illinois regiment, saying that he preferred to remain in the ranks of the 76th. Then, as alleged in the complaint, Col. Busey caused him to be tied by the wrists to a tree for refusing to obey the order.

Brig. Gen. Christopher Andrews responded to the complaint by advising Col. Busey that the "detailing of an enlisted man to serve in another regiment is unauthorized." The colonel replied that he believed that regimental commanders had such authority, because divisional commanders "to which we have formerly been attached allowed such an exchange."

March–April 1865
Second Inaugural Address; From Florida to Fort Blakely

On March 4, President Lincoln gave his second inaugural address. It should be read in its entirety, so I will not quote from it.

Pvt. Moses Spain of Company E died of disease (inflammation of the lungs) at Memphis on March 7.

On March 11, the 76th moved to Pensacola. In late March and early April, it traveled from Pensacola toward Spanish Fort and Fort Blakely, near Mobile, Alabama. Many years later, Second Lt. William Kenaga, Company I, recounted his personal recollections of that time:

Second Lt. William Kenaga
Kankakee, Illinois
(3rd Reunion of Survivors 64 [1888])

Starting from Pensacola, Florida, we arrived at the little village of Stockton, situated on the east bank of the Alabama river, about 15 miles above the old village of Blakely, on the 31st day of March, 1865. We had been enroute in the Florida swamps twelve days on half rations and no rations. A glimpse of civilization and a prospect of getting something to eat made glad the hearts of all. While on this march one day's experience differed but little from another, with the enemy constantly in our front,

bridges destroyed, an unusual amount of rain and overflowing of the whole county, made the roads much of the way impassable except where we bridged or corduroyed, for this purpose we had on either side of the road an abundance of pine trees from six to twelve inches through, which were used with an unsparing hand. While nearing Stockton we passed the first forage enroute, it was corn in the crib, and like the "Pied Piper of Hamlin," we piped and our empty haversacks were filled with ear corn and we were happy. We had been hearing heavy cannonading for the past ten days. April 1st, our force, consisting of about 13,000 men under Maj. Gen. Steele, proceeded down the river toward Blakely over an old and well constructed highway, rolling country and much of the land of an excellent quality. [T]he Seventy-sixth, being the rear guard that day, did not leave Stockton until after noon. We then made about 13 miles and when within possibly one mile of the fort near Blakely, we filed to the left of the Stockton road, through a dense forest, possibly eighty rods, (the night was intensely dark) with shot and shell from fort and gunboats dropping here and there and screeching over our heads like skyrockets at a Fourth of July celebration, we halted, and to prevent our exact location from being discovered, we were forbidden to kindle a fire.

About eleven o'clock we changed our position back toward the Stockton road, and had just finished being aligned and given orders to lay down on our arms, when shell after shell in rapid succession passed a few feet in our immediate front, our position was changed a few rods to the left and rear, where the regiment remained during the siege, fully protected by an abrupt elevation of possibly forty feet (5th Reunion of Survivors 33-40 [1890]).

Union soldiers under the command of Maj. Gen. Edward Canby initiated a siege of Spanish Fort on March 27, and they captured it on April 8.

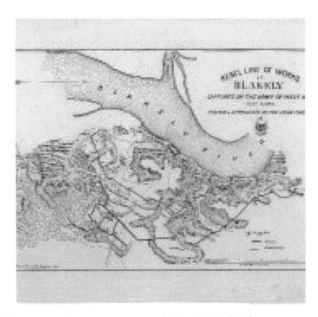

Map showing Fort Blakely, Alabama, on April 9, 1865; Union army positions are colored blue; Confederate works are colored red

Map courtesy Library of Virginia

(Cited as "United States Army Corps of Engineers" in the bibliography)

In the east on April 9, Gen. Robert E. Lee surrendered the Army of Northern Virginia to Gen. Grant at Appomattox.

After a siege of eight days, Col. Busey led the 76th in the assault on Fort Blakely during late afternoon on April 9, charging through *abatis* and heavy gunfire. The entire Confederate garrison was captured.

Maj. Matthew Peters from Watseka, Illinois (although during the war a member of the 74th Ohio Volunteer Infantry Regiment), provided a graphic description of the Confederate defenses:

The confederate line of forts to be assaulted were nine in number, located in a semi-circle extending from river to river and connected with heavy breastworks covering a distance of two miles or more. The earth from which the breastworks were constructed left a ditch or trench (in military parlance "a moat") in front. About two hundred yards in front of these forts and breastworks were a series of rifle-pits covering the entire line; in these pits were sheltered the enemy's sharpshooters. Still in front of these about fifty yards was the abattis consisting of trees felled outward with their branches woven together and wires wound through to hold these branches firmly in place. Between the rifle-pits and abattis the timber had been cut down and left a tangled mass of stumps, logs and limbs, the purpose being to obstruct passage and give the sharpshooters in the pits a better opportunity to repulse any attack upon the forts (Kern 1907, 692).

Brig. Gen. (Brevet Maj. Gen.) Christopher Andrews participated in the siege and storming of Fort Blakely as commander of the 2nd Division of the 13th Army Corps. After the war, he wrote the *History of the Campaign of Mobile*, which included a lengthy description of the attack by the 76th on fort number three of the nine forts referred to by Maj. Peters:

The Seventy-sixth Illinois charged directly on the redoubt in their front, the one north of the Stockton road, and preserved its alignment well till it got to the second line of abatis. One man of that regiment was killed at the first line of abatis and rifle-pits; then, at the second line, the battle became fierce and bloody. The confederates maintained a bold front from behind their breastworks, and when the Seventy-sixth was within fifty yards of the redoubt, they suffered severely from the confederate musketry and artillery. While a part of the regiment maintained a spirited fire, the rest crossed the abatis. Lieut. Wm. F. Kenaga was shot through a leg at the second abatis, and nearer the works was hit in the ankle-joint of his other leg; then, unable to walk, he kept upright on his knees and rallied and cheered the men. The color sergeant, [Henry] Hussey, was killed within twenty feet of the works; then the colors were taken by the noble and brave Corporal Goldwood, who, as he was planting them on the parapet, received the contents of three muskets so close that the discharge burnt his clothes, and he fell dead inside the works with the colors in his arms.

The Seventy-sixth and the confederates were now fighting across the works, and those of the regiment in the rear were coming up as fast as they could pass the obstructions. Col. Busey ran along close to the parapet, and, with his revolver, disabled the gunner of a howitzer about to be fired, and which afterward proved to have a double charge of grape and canister; then turning to the right, he exchanged shots with two at short range. Afterward, he ordered Lieut.-Col. Jones, with Capts. Hughes and Ingerson [Ingersoll], and Lieut. Warner, with from twenty to fifty men, to charge the right flank of the redoubt, while he, with another squad, charged the front. They charged with bayonets, and drove the confederates from the works.

Fifty yards in rear of the redoubt the ground began to slope considerably. It had been cleared of thick underbrush, and the latter had been piled in a row along the crest. Behind that cover the confederates formed again, and gave another volley, wounding, among others, Col. Busey and Capt. Hughes. Then the Seventy-sixth charged them again, and they threw down their arms, and ran into the woods and toward the landing. Col. Busey sent detachments in pursuit of them. Upward of four hundred prisoners fell into the possession of the Seventy-sixth. It had five men killed inside the works. Its whole number of killed was sixteen, of whom, besides those already mentioned, were Sergeant Perkins and Corporals Hopkins and Tremain. There were eighty wounded, some mortally; so that its entire casualties were about one hundred. Among the wounded were Lieuts. Martin and Warner. The Seventy-sixth Illinois entered the works over the south salient of the redoubt, and over the breastworks extending south. Its national colors were planted on the breastwork. It was claimed by his comrades that Private Eldrick Bromillet, of Company D, was the first one of the regiment over the works. He was killed fifty yards inside the works by a confederate captain, and the latter was killed by Bromillet's comrade. That regiment used the bayonet in the charge, and displayed throughout the highest degree of valor. No regiment on the field that day suffered so heavily, none exhibited more intrepid bravery. And higher praise than that cannot be awarded troops.

All this occurred on the same day that Gen. Lee surrendered to Gen. Grant at Appomattox.

Col. Busey received a flesh wound in the left thigh. He was later appointed brevet brigadier general for "gallant conduct in leading his regiment in the assault on Fort Blakely, Alabama."

April 1865
Assassination

On April 14, President Abraham Lincoln was shot at Ford's Theater in Washington, DC, and he died the following day. He is buried in Oak Ridge Cemetery, Springfield, Illinois, about 107 miles' straight-line distance from Ash Grove.

You had gathered soldiers

in the East and West,

and gave the task to Generals

to defeat the Rebels

and subdue the defiant States.

You dwell now

in the heaven of our minds,

and we go on longing for you,

regardless of the passing

of the years.

Charles M. Brock

The men of the 76th did not learn of the President's death until April 20, because of downed telegraph wires.

Before the war, Franklin Blades, regimental surgeon of the 76th Illinois. had been elected twice to the Illinois House of Representatives, in 1856 and 1860,and he was an acquaintance of Abraham Lincoln's. In later life, Judge Blades—he was both a doctor and a lawyer—wrote down some of his recollections of Lincoln. Here are two:

(1) In the Spring of 1858, having been admitted to the bar, and intending to give up the profession of medicine, I wrote to Mr. Lincoln, requesting the use of his name as a reference on my professional card as a lawyer. He had known me as a physician, and in writing to him I said nothing about my change of profession, and so in replying he seemed to be in doubt as to whether I was the same Blades he had known. So he wrote: "I do not know whether you are Dr. Blades or not. If you are Dr. Blades, you may use my name; if you are not Dr. Blades, if Dr. Blades says you may use my name, you may do so."

(2) People of a later generation can have no adequate appreciation of the intense hostility, and even hatred, with which Mr. Lincoln was regarded by his political opponents. We who lived then and were heartily with him in his efforts to maintain the Union could see, and did see, that many of them exulted when they heard that he was killed. They dared not much to show it, else they themselves would have been killed. Blinded by intense partisan spirit, and blind to the fact that the slave power had long been planning either to make it lawful to carry their slaves into every quarter of the Union or to dissolve the Union, they laid the whole trouble at the door of those who were simply resisting the further extension of slavery. (Cited as "*Abraham Lincoln, By Some Men Who Knew Him*" in the bibliography.)

April–July 1865
Mustering Out at Galveston, Texas; Return to Illinois

After the capture of Fort Blakely, the regiment moved to Mobile. From there it was transported to Selma, Alabama, followed by a return to Mobile.

In May, Silas's cousin, Sgt. Thomas Roberts of Company K, was promoted to first lieutenant in Mobile. Roberts was absent sick in a Mobile hospital in May and June. He assumed command on July 13.

Pvt. Harvey Longnecker of Company E died of disease (typhoid fever) at Mobile on June 1.

The 76th embarked on the steamship *Herman Livingston* across the Gulf of Mexico to Galveston, Texas, in late June. Silas, John Gilbert, Thomas Roberts, and the other members of the 76th were mustered out on July 22. Silas's service record noted that he was due a bounty of $75 and a clothing allowance of $12.54, and that he owed $6 for "arms, equipments, etc." The 76th then traveled to New Orleans, by boat to Cairo and by rail to Chicago, where the regiment was disbanded on August 4.

According to the Illinois adjutant general's report, the 76th Illinois traveled over ten thousand miles during its three years of service. Beckwith says the distance was over twelve thousand miles.

1865
Thirteenth Amendment

Congress passed the Thirteenth Amendment to the Constitution, abolishing the evil of slavery nationwide, on January 31, 1865. The states ratified it on December 6, 1865. On February 1, 1865, Illinois was the first state to ratify the amendment.

Chapter 11

In Memoriam

Monument to First Lt. Peter Williams and the 76th Illinois in Vicksburg

As recounted in chapter 8, First Lt. Peter Williams of Company E, preacher of the Methodist Episcopal Church in Milford, Illinois, was shot while on picket duty and died during the "investment" (siege) of Vicksburg, on June 21, 1863.

The Milford Church has lost
its minister, its leading light.
His congregation prayed
when Williams passed away.

"Lead, Kindly Light,
amid the encircling gloom,
Lead Thou me on!
The night is dark,
and I am far from home—
Lead Thou me on!"

They prayed this war
would end, they prayed
that war would disappear
and peace would be decreed.

Charles M. Brock

This is a photograph from the proceedings of the 20th Reunion of Survivors (1906).   The State of Illinois erected this monument to the 76th Illinois and First Lt. Peter Williams at Vicksburg in 1907, the site being the position occupied by the regiment at the surrender of Vicksburg on July 4, 1863. Col. Busey stood near the monument on the day it was dedicated. Source: Local History and Genealogy Collection, Peoria Public Library, Peoria, Illinois.

Monument to the 76th Illinois and Lt. Peter Williams at Vicksburg

This is another photograph of the same monument to the 76th Illinois and First Lt. Williams, placed outside of Vicksburg National Military Park on former park property in the city of Vicksburg, fifty yards north of Illinois Circle (north) on Hall's Ferry Road.   Following is the inscription:

76th INFANTRY

COL. SAMUEL T. BUSEY,
2ND BRIG., 4TH DIV, 16TH CORPS,

ENTERED CAMPAIGN
AT YOUNG'S POINT,
LOUISIANA, ABOUT MAY 15, 1863.
INVESTMENT LINE ABOUT MAY 25.

CASUALTIES:
DURING SIEGE,
LIEUT. PETER J. WILLIAMS
MORTALLY WOUNDED.

(Cited as "United States National Park Service. *Vicksburg National Military Park, Mississippi—76th Illinois Infantry"* in the bibliography.)

Monument in the Mobile National Cemetery, Mobile, Alabama, to the 76th Illinois Soldiers Buried in That Cemetery

Mobile National Cemetery, Mobile, Alabama
Monument to the 76th Illinois Soldiers Buried in That Cemetery

(Cited as "Fraser, Clayton B." in the bibliography)

The Mobile National Cemetery in Mobile, Alabama, includes a monument dedicated to fallen soldiers of the 76th Illinois. The regiment's survivors funded the erection of the marble monument in 1892. The monument bears the names of the twenty-nine members of the 76th buried in the Mobile cemetery, including those killed in the assault on Fort Blakely. The members from Ash Grove buried at Mobile include Sgt. William Duke (the mechanic from Manchester, England, who was wounded at Fort Blakely and who died sometime later), Pvt. Harvey Longnecker (died of disease June 1 at Mobile), and Sgt. Henry Hussey (killed in the assault on Fort Blakely). On the front of the shaft is the following dedication:

IN MEMORY

OF OUR HEROES WHO FELL AT

FORT BLAKELY, ALA.,

APRIL 9, 1865.

————

ERECTED BY

THE SURVIVORS OF THE

REGIMENT.

————

1892.

State of Illinois Memorial Temple in Vicksburg National Military Park

The proceedings of the 21st Reunion of Survivors (1907) included this photograph of the State of Illinois Memorial Temple at Vicksburg, which was dedicated on October 26, 1906. It was built of white Georgia marble at a cost of $200,000. Those proceedings also included a report by a committee who visited Vicksburg in 1904 in order to locate the last camp occupied by the 76th regiment during the siege. Col. Busey made the following statement at the reunion:

> My regiment…enjoys the distinction of being the only one in the siege that camped inside of what is now the government reservation. We were closer to the Confederate forts than any other regiment on that part of the line and were out in the open and within 150 yards of the Confederate guns.

Capt. N. A. Riley of Company B said:

> Very few people living can comprehend what a vast undertaking the capture of Vicksburg was. General U. S. Grant always regarded his Vicksburg campaign as the most brilliant and strategic of all his campaigns. To know just what was accomplished one must go over the ground and view the wonderful natural fortifications. Looking over the situation now after forty years one is inclined to the belief that with abundant provisions and ammunition Vicksburg might have held out for many months longer and perhaps compelled General Grant to have raised the siege.

Sgt. Maj. Munhall confirmed that the memorial included a bronze tablet embedded in the wall, containing the names of every officer and soldier of the 76th who participated in the siege and capture of Vicksburg. **Source: Local History and Genealogy Collection, Peoria Public Library, Peoria, Illinois.**

Here are current views of the monument, from the National Park Service website. "There are forty-seven steps in the long stairway, one for each day of the Siege of Vicksburg. Modeled after the Roman Pantheon, the monument has sixty unique bronze tablets lining its interior walls, naming all 36,325 Illinois soldiers who participated in the Vicksburg Campaign."

(Cited as "United States National Park Service. *Vicksburg National Military Park, Mississippi—Illinois Memorial"* in the bibliography.)

Monument to Civil War Soldiers in the GAR Cemetery, Watseka, Illinois

In 1893, the Williams Post No. 25 GAR erected a monument to Civil War soldiers in the GAR Cemetery in Watseka, Illinois.

Remembrance of Ash Grove Men

Of the seventeen Ash Grove men assigned to the 76th, Company E, two—John Keady and Charles Longnecker—were discharged for disability in 1863; seven died:

Benjamin Bratton died of disease
      (febris typhoid)
at La Grange, Tennessee,
on March 18, 1863
Widow—Delilah
Child—Addison

James Higginson died of disease (chronic
      diarrhea)
at Natchez, Mississippi,
on November 24, 1863

Harvey Longnecker died of disease
      (typhoid fever)
at Mobile, Alabama,
on June 1, 1865
(buried in Mobile National
Cemetery, Mobile, Alabama)

Joseph McKinley died on March 20, 1865
at Ash Grove
of wounds suffered in action
near Jackson, Mississippi,
on July 7, 1864

Samuel Montgomery died on July 11, 1864
in the hospital
of wounds suffered in action
near Jackson, Mississippi,
on July 7, 1864
Father—John
Mother—Elizabeth
Siblings—James, Daniel, Charles,
   Julia, and Peter
(buried in Pitchin Cemetery)

Hamilton Spain died of disease (pneumonia)
at La Grange, Tennessee,
on December 17, 1862
(buried in Memphis National
Cemetery, Memphis, Tennessee)

Moses Spain died of disease (inflammation
        of the lungs)
at Memphis, Tennessee,
on March 7, 1865
Widow—Elizabeth
Child—Francis
(buried in Memphis National
Cemetery, Memphis, Tennessee)

Of the twenty-nine Ash Grove men in the 76th, Company K, six were discharged for disability—Capt. Joseph Davis, Pvt. Lorenzo Honn, Pvt. Nelson Jenkins, Pvt. John Linball, Sgt. Green Neeld, and Pvt. Robert Teeter; one was transferred to the veteran reserve corps—Pvt. Benjamin South; and twelve died:

Elijah Bratten was killed in action
near Jackson, Mississippi,
on July 7, 1864

Jonathan Clawson died of disease (pneumonia)
at La Grange, Tennessee,
on December 4, 1862
Widow—Lucy
Children—Delphine, Freeman,
        and John (son Abraham
        dead at five months in 1860
        and buried in Pitchin Cemetery)

William Duke was wounded
at Fort Blakely, Alabama,
and subsequently died
(buried in Mobile National
Cemetery, Mobile, Alabama)

Hiram Harris died of disease (unstated)
at Oxford, Mississippi,
on December 17, 1862
Siblings—David, William, and
        Rebecca
(buried in abandoned cemetery
next to Mud Creek in Ash Grove,
once a family burying ground)

Elisha Hawkins was killed in action
near Jackson, Mississippi,
on July 7, 1864
Father—Joseph
Mother—Ellenor

Henry Hussey was killed in action
at Fort Blakely, Alabama,
on April 9, 1865
Widow—Lidy
(buried in Mobile National
Cemetery, Mobile, Alabama)

Oliver Nail died from effects of a kick
      by a horse
at Columbus, Kentucky,
on October 5, 1862
(buried in Pitchin Cemetery)

Samuel Rowley was killed in action
near Jackson, Mississippi,
on July 7, 1864

Aaron Russell died of disease (measles)
at La Grange, Tennessee,
on November 16, 1862

George Thomas died of disease (measles)
at La Grange, Tennessee,
on December 2 or 5, 1862
(buried in Memphis National
 Cemetery, Memphis, Tennessee)

Isaac VanHorn died of disease (catarrh)
at Memphis, Tennessee,
on February 21, 1863
Widow—Eliza

Joel Vaughn died of disease (chronic diarrhea)
at St. Louis, Missouri,
on April 11 or 18, 1863
Father—John
Mother—Esther
Siblings—Delight and Vephanel

Of the thirty-three Ash Grove men identified in regiments other than the 76th, one soldier—Silas Harris of the 113th—was discharged for disability in 1863; and three died:

> Thomas Cady of the 12th Illinois
> was wounded at the Battle of Corinth
> on October 4, 1862
> and died at St. Louis, Missouri,
> on November 13, 1862
> Father—John
> Mother—Ellen
> Brothers—Robert and David
> Sister—Mary Ellen Esabella
>
> Morris Neighbor of the 25th
> was killed in action
> at Pea Ridge, Arkansas,
> on March 8, 1862
>
> David Swank of the 113th
> died of disease
> at Onarga, Illinois,
> on October 2, 1862
> (buried in Pitchin Cemetery)

In total, of the seventy-nine Ash Grove men identified in the Illinois State Archives, twenty-two died during the war—thirteen from disease and nine from combat. Nine men were discharged for disability.

Pvt. John Wesley Nunamaker, a son of one of the two earliest settlers of Ash Grove, John Nunamaker, died near Kingston, Georgia, in September 1864. A memorial marker was placed for Nunamaker in Hickory Point Cemetery, Warren County, Illinois. Sometime later, his parents moved to Indianola, Warren County, Iowa.

> Pvt. John Wesley Nunamaker
> of the 84th Illinois
> died near Kingston, Georgia,
> on September 23, 1864

Musicians played "The Vacant Chair":

> *We shall meet, but we shall miss him,*
> *There will be one vacant chair*
> *We shall linger to caress him*
> *While we breathe our evening prayer.*

Chapter 12

Ash Grove in the Postwar Years

Silas Brock and His Family Following the Civil War

After the war, Silas continued farming in Ash Grove for about twelve years. In 1877, he moved into Pitchin. He worked in a drugstore until the late 1880s, when he opened his own drugstore, and several years later a general merchandise establishment.

All of Silas and Maria's children were born and raised in Ash Grove. Mary was born in 1866, Bertha in 1868, Rose in 1871, and my grandfather Marquis Amos ("Mark") in 1874. Both Bertha and Rose died before I was born in 1941. But I knew Mary ("Aunt May") and Mark quite well.

All four children attended the Glenwood School in Ash Grove, and the Grand Prairie Seminary and Commercial College in Onarga, Illinois, about twenty miles northwest of Ash Grove.

The seminary was a private, co-educational boarding school. Ministers of the Methodist Episcopal Church and others from a number of nearby villages, including Kankakee and Middleport (now Watseka), incorporated it in 1863 at the height of the Civil War. The school's trustees built a three-story building in 1864. The initial tuition charge ranged from $2 to $12 depending upon the courses selected. (Cited as "Frazer, Todd M." in the bibliography.)

In 1899, Silas and Maria moved about ten miles to Cissna Park, where he opened a drugstore with son Mark.

Their daughter Rose was widowed in 1904. She and her five children, the oldest of whom was ten, then went to live with Silas and Maria, who, as a result, helped to raise a second family. Rose later assisted her father in the drug store.

Silas had a strong sense of public service. He served as justice of the peace in Ash Grove for twelve years. He also held the offices of township collector, assessor, and postmaster at various times.

Silas didn't believe in locked doors. When he built his home in Cissna Park, he had wax put in the keyholes of all the outside doors.

Aunt May married Austin Pierce, a jeweler, in 1885. He died in 1923. When I knew her, she was already in her eighties. I remember a tall, white-haired woman, slightly stoop-shouldered, with deep-set eyes like her paternal grandmother, Mary Ann Bishop. Aunt May lived in a small single-story house in the town of Milford, about fifteen miles east of Ash Grove, with two of her three children. Homer was a widower, and Edith never married. Her third child, Silas, died in 1951. I found Aunt May to be a warm, caring person. She died in 1960 at ninety-four.

Mark married Mabel Westgate in 1901, and they had two children, Donald and my father, Glen. When I knew him, Grandfather was already in his seventies, a tall, dignified, but amiable man with deep-set eyes like his sister Mary. A drunk driver killed Grandmother in an auto accident in 1946. I remember the telephone call my father received about the accident as if it were yesterday. After that, Grandfather lived with us in Watseka for a number of years. He remarried in 1950, but his second wife, Grace, died in 1953. Then he came back to live with us. He would occasionally bring us produce—such as a bushel of sweet corn, fresh strawberries, or rich thick cream—from farms around Cissna Park.

During summers I would frequently drive him from Watseka to his accounting office in Cissna Park. He never discussed his early years in Ash Grove or his parents with me, and I never had the foresight to ask him questions. He died in 1959 at eighty-four, seven months before I left home for Princeton.

My father established his law practice in Watseka in the 1930s. During World War II, when he was a special agent in the Federal Bureau of Investigation, we lived in Louisville, Kentucky, and Cleveland, Ohio. We didn't return to Watseka until 1945, so I have few recollections of Grandmother. I remember sitting with her in a car in front of the general store in Claytonville, a tiny village near Ash Grove where they lived and where my father had been born. As we sat there together, she taught me the words of "My Darling Clementine." She was a tiny, exuberant, outgoing woman who was active in community and women's affairs. That song runs through my head on an almost daily basis, even after seventy years.

My father's brother, Uncle Don, served in the army during World War II in Africa, Italy, and France. He was discharged without injury with the rank of lieutenant colonel. The two brothers shared a cordial relationship, but for some unexplained reason, they were not close.

My fondest boyhood recollection of my father's law practice involved payments in kind he received from several elderly women clients—payments in the form of cookies, pies, and homemade bread, especially the homemade bread. My brothers and I would devour it warm, smothered in melted butter, in one sitting. Perhaps that was the inspiration behind my choice of career.

Pitchin and the "Iron Horse"—Disruptive Technology (1882)

Pitchin no longer exists. It vanished because, in 1882, the Chicago & Eastern Illinois Railroad opened an eleven-mile spur from a spot just north of Wellington (called "Cissna Junction") to Cissna Park, about seven miles southwest of Pitchin. It handled both freight—livestock, grain, etc.—and passengers. Locals nicknamed the train the "Backup" because it had no turntable.

Having the train come in was a triumph, and every time it came in everybody who had time met the train twice a day. It pulled out at 6 o'clock in the morning and backed in at noon, pulled out again at 1 o'clock and backed back in again around 6 in the evening….The train consisted of an engine, a coal car, a passenger car and a caboose, plus grain or cattle cars that would be added. Passenger service was satisfactory on any train. One could get on the train in the morning, get on the mail train at Wellington, go to Watseka, come back on the mail train at 3 o'clock and ride back to Cissna Park, a day's shopping done. Or one could go to Hoopeston and shop or on to Danville to spend the day. The passenger trains were plentiful on the C & E I. Riding on the branch train was always a social event, too. Everybody knew everybody else and it was a nice visiting occasion. Sometimes even romances started on the train. It wasn't a smooth ride, for switching cars and coupling grain or coal cars gave one a most distinct jolt; but even that was fun sometimes.

That is from "The Early History of Cissna Park, Illinois," by Tylla Herman Landes, an unpublished document which I discovered in my father's files. She moved with her family from Pitchin to Cissna Park in 1893. Other Pitchin residents eventually moved to Cissna Park as well.

The Colony as of 1884

Fifty years after Lewis Roberts and John Hunnel made their initial land purchases in Ash Grove, the original Roberts/Brock/Cady colony no longer existed, only a few members of the colony remained.

Wesley Harvey farmed in Ash Grove until his health failed him, although he continued to own farmland as of 1884. He operated a mercantile business in Pitchin from 1866 to 1870, and then again beginning in 1876. He held various public offices in Pitchin, including justice of the peace, supervisor, and assessor. In 1890, Wesley and Mary Ann sold the farm and moved to Cissna Park, where Wesley opened the Wesley Harvey and Son General Store. His son Henry, Silas's stepbrother, ran the store with Wesley as a nominal partner. Wesley died in 1893 and Mary Ann in 1897.

John Willoughby was still farming in Ash Grove in 1884. His wife, Polly Brock, Silas's aunt, had died in 1854. John Willoughby died in 1892. Several Willoughbys (perhaps grandchildren) are named as landowners in Section 22 on the map on the next page.

E

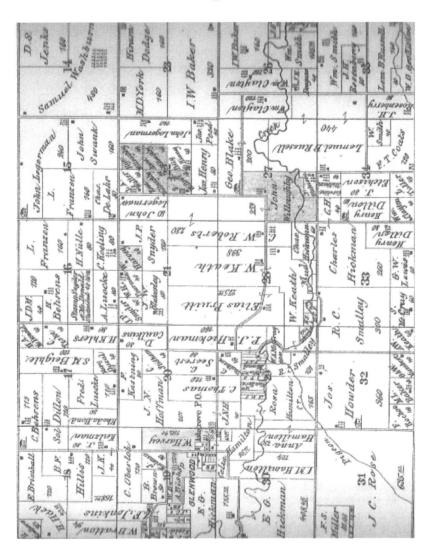

Ash Grove in 1884
(Cited as "Atlas Map Iroquois County, Illinois" in the bibliography)

Lewis Roberts Jr., a Methodist minister, Methodist minister, was living in Peru, Indiana, as of 1884.

George and Lewis Nunamaker, sons of John Nunamaker and Catharine Roberts, were alive as of 1884. Their parents were both deceased.

Elizabeth Harvey left Ash Grove sometime after the death of her husband George Allen in 1849 and moved to Greencastle, Indiana, where her son Marquis Lewis was attending Indiana Asbury University. She was alive in 1884, as were her children, Marquis Lewis and Mary.

Marquis Lewis was a teacher at the Illinois Institution for the Education of the Deaf and Dumb in Jacksonville, Illinois, from 1858 to 1869, and from 1875 to 1893. He founded the Deaf and Dumb Institute of Arkansas in 1869. From 1870 to 1875, he was an instructor in the Pennsylvania Deaf and Dumb Institute. He married Elvira Gage in

1871. She was a teacher at the Jacksonville institution from 1860 to 1871. They had no children.

John Cady was still farming on 80 acres in Iroquois County (Artesia Township) as of 1884 (not shown on the above map).

Of the 57 men from Ash Grove who enlisted in the Union army and who survived the war, only three, including Silas, were still living in Ash Grove as of 1884. Thomas Roberts, Silas's cousin, was living in Onarga.

Chapter 13

Family Album

Mary Ann Bishop
(Silas Brock's mother)

Wesley Harvey
(Silas Brock's stepfather)

Marquis Lewis Brock
(Silas's cousin)

Photograph courtesy The Fraternity of Phi Gamma Delta
(Cited as "Blackstock" in the bibliography)

Silas Brock

Silas and Maria Brock

Marquis (Mark), Rose, Silas, Maria, Mary L. (May) BROCK

Silas Brock, Company E, 76th Illinois Volunteer Infantry

Photograph courtesy Doris Kogler

Mabel and Mark Brock

Lucile and Glen Brock

My father practiced law in Watseka for sixty years, except during the years of World War II, when he was a special agent for the Federal Bureau of Investigation. Silas knew my father during the first twenty years of his life, and I have no doubt that Silas perceived in him then the qualities that would make him the extraordinary individual who he was.   I also have no doubt that my father inherited many of those qualities from Silas and from Mark, his father, strong moral character, perseverance, belief in education, family orientation, dedication to community, and respect for the dignity of individuals.

Following are two resolutions regarding my father, the first adopted by the Iroquois County Bar Association on December 1, 1999, and the second adopted by the Iroquois Federal Savings and Loan Association of Watseka on November 9, 1999, shortly after his death. Silas would have been proud of him.

RESOLUTION

WHEREAS, GLEN W. BROCK'S life came to a close on the 18th day of October, 1999; and

WHEREAS, the members of the Iroquois County Bar Association desire to make a matter of record their sentiments regarding the life of Glen W. Brock,

IT IS THEREFORE RESOLVED by the Iroquois County Bar Association:

1. That Glen W. Brock, as a private practitioner for more than sixty years, was always considered by the legal profession throughout our State, County, and wherever he was known, as a lawyer of extraordinary ability;

2. That Glen W. Brock's professional career was characterized by fairness, honesty, loyalty, and faithfulness to his clients;

3. That Glen W. Brock loved life, and was a dedicated family man, having been married to Lucille for almost sixty years, and having raised four sons who have become significant citizens in their communities;

4. That Glen W. Brock was a leader in the financial development of Iroquois County as President, Chairman and Director of Iroquois Federal Savings and Loan Association;

5. That a copy of these observations be made a matter of record in the Court of Record in Iroquois County, Illinois, and that a copy be furnished to Glen W. Brock's family and to the news media.

PASSED unanimously at the meeting of the Iroquois County Bar Association on December 1, 1999.

James L. Tungate, President

Attest: Hon. David A. Youck, Secretary

CONDOLENCE RESOLUTION: Secretary Heuton read the following Resolution:

<u>CONDOLENCE RESOLUTION</u>

We wish to recognize the services of Glen W Brock as a Director and Director Emeritus of this Association from the date of his election to the Board of Directors on February 12, 1946 until his death on Monday, October 18, 1999. Director Brock served as President of Iroquois Federal Savings and Loan Association from 1953 to 1974 at which time he was elected Chairman of the Board of Directors. Mr. Brock served as Chairman until 1978 when he retired as an active board member. He brought to the Board a considerable knowledge of legal and commercial affairs, and had a wide public acquaintance. He was regular in attendance, missing no meetings unless prevented by illness, and he served on many committees. Throughout this long service his attitude, expressions, and decisions in relation to finances and public relations entitle him to no small credit for the growth from $1,600,000 to $284,000,000 in assets of the Association during his years of friendly cooperation in matters of directorate concern.

THEREFORE BE IT RESOLVED by the Board of Directors of Iroquois Federal Savings and Loan Association that the above and the foregoing be made an integral part of this Resolution; that our sincere and deep sympathy be extended to the bereaved family of our late associate, and that a copy hereof be sent to his wife, Lucile Brock and to his children, Charles M. Brock, James R. Brock, Thomas W. Brock, and Stephen L. Brock.

Director Gary Martin moved that the above Resolution be adopted. Seconded by Director Sunderland. Motion carried on roll call.

Dated this 9th day of November, 1999

IROQUOIS FEDERAL SAVINGS AND LOAN ASSOCIATION

201 EAST CHERRY STREET • P.O. BOX 190 • WATSEKA, ILLINOIS 60970-0190 • 815/432-2476
BRANCH OFFICE: 819 N. GILBERT ST. • P. O. BOX 1277 • DANVILLE, IL 61834-1277 • 217/446-0184
BRANCH OFFICE: 175 E. FOURTH ST. • P. O. BOX 605 • CLIFTON, IL 60927-0605 • 815/694-2315
BRANCH OFFICE: 511 S. CHICAGO RD. • P.O. BOX 385 • HOOPESTON, IL 60942-0365 • 217/283-5134

My father was interested in family history. He and my mother were both intensely family oriented. And, according to my youngest brother, Steve (fifteen years younger than I), he had an interest in Pitchin. As Steve wrote to me: "I remember Dad and Mom taking me there at least twice, maybe more. I think we went at least once with Edith Pierce [Aunt May's daughter]. Maybe with others too? I don't remember. But I mention it because I think it confirms that as he got older, Dad did take more of an interest in these things." I guess Steve was suggesting, in his own subtle way, that I, now seventy-four, am going through the same phase by writing this story.

I believe my father might have become a Methodist minister had he not been driven by intense ambition to pursue the practice of law. Every Saturday evening for many years, he spent several hours on the phone with Rev. Ernest Duling of the Watseka Methodist Church discussing the next day's sermon.

My father was also a lover of poetry. He often recited favorite lines, such as Robert Burns's "To a Mouse, on Turning Her Up in Her Nest with the Plough":

> Wee, sleekit, cow'rin, tim'rous beastie,
> O, what a panic's in thy breastie!
> Thou need na start awa sae hasty
> Wi bickering brattle!
> I wad be laith to rin an' chase thee,
> Wi' murdering pattle....
>
> Still thou are blest, compared wi' me!
> The present only toucheth thee:
> But och! I backward cast my e'e,
> On prospects drear!
> An' forward, tho' I canna see,
> I guess an' fear!

And such as William Cullen Bryant's "Thanatopsis":

> Yet a few days, and thee
> The all-beholding sun shall see no more
> In all his course....

And "The Pillar of Cloud" by John Henry Cardinal Newman, quoted in Chapter 11.

He and my mother believed absolutely in the value of education, and both were voracious readers. He put himself through the University of Illinois by waiting on tables. It appears his ancestors, such as Silas and Mary Ann, and George Allen Brock and Elizabeth Harvey, also believed in education. But most of them, except for Marquis Lewis Brock, had meager educational opportunities.

Postscript on Pioneering

After forty years spent traveling the world, I come back to Silas and Ash Grove, one hundred fifty years after the end of the incredibly brutal Civil War and eighty-eight years after his death. I am in awe of Bishop Roberts, a pioneer of the church, and the pioneer prairie farmers in this story, in awe of their perseverance and their ability to cope with adversity. But what does a male-oriented community of white, Methodist, Whig/Republican prairie farmers—a community of faith—have to say to our world, where the dominant modality is diverse, secular, urban, family-scattered, equality-driven, politically and culturally divisive?

From the perspective of a prairie farmer/Civil War veteran/druggist, the twentieth was a century of miraculous human achievement—pioneering in many fields—and massive human brutality on a global scale. And Silas witnessed only the first quarter of it, including the Great War. I have my own epitaph for the century:

Pour une âme melée aux affaires lointaines
The immediate with its multiple
Mirrors, instantaneous replays,
The frozen moments iterated
To a tropical intensity
Pour une âme melée aux affaires lointaines
We have replaced the image of perfection
With the perfecting of an image,
Vision with television,
Clarity with clarification,
The ultimate with the ultimatum,
Harmony with harmonization,
Deliverance with delivery systems,
Pour une âme melée aux affaires lointaines
Perception with process.
We have accomplished most and may be worst
Remembered. We who first walked the heavens,
We who have piped our music to the stars,
Will leave what vestige in a trail of blood?
Pour une âme melée aux affaires lointaines.

Charles M. Brock

As I write this Internet-enabled book on my iMac, I'm also listening to CNN talk about NASA's launch of a new Orion spacecraft from Cape Canaveral. The reporter said NASA hopes this flight will usher in a new era in spaceflight, with eventual human explorations of the asteroids and Mars. If you imagine a straight line from Earth to Mars, it measures *on average* about 140,000,000 miles. Of course, the flight path through the forest of dark will hardly be in a straight line.

From my perspective, the contrast between our world and the life of the early nineteenth-century prairie farmer is breathtaking. And the glorious human pioneering spirit remains alive! May it live forever! Three cheers for the human race! Or, as members of the 76th Illinois Regiment would have said, "Three cheers and a tiger!

The Earth may live

The Earth may die

But women and men

Will climb the sky.

There's a new thing there

That's under that sun,

Or beyond that star,

Or is it all one?

And remember

The darkness, the dark in space,

For it will be

Endless…endless.

Ransack the asteroids,

Settle the Moon,

Colonize Mars.

And the race is on!

Bread upon waters,

Rockets into space.

Then discover the Earth,

That beginning place.

Let the Earth be heaven,

And the heavens

Multifoliate Earth,

For reverent humans.

Then the Earth shall live

And all shall be seen,

And this universe

Shall be evergreen.

Then the Earth shall thrive

Like a tree by the stream

That all living things

May share in the dream.

Charles M. Brock

Appendix 1

Family Trees (Partial)

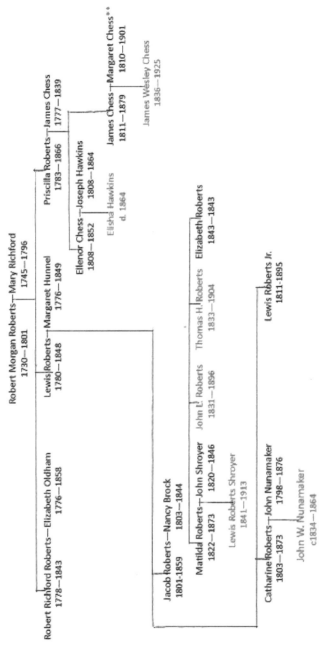

Appendix 1
Family Trees
Roberts Family Tree (Partial)*

* Based upon family history/genealogy information in Find A Grave (http://www.findagrave.com)

NOTE: The six men highlighted in red served in the Union army during the Civil War.

** Margaret Chess's son from a prior marriage, William Gasaway (d. 1863), also served in the Union army during the Civil War.

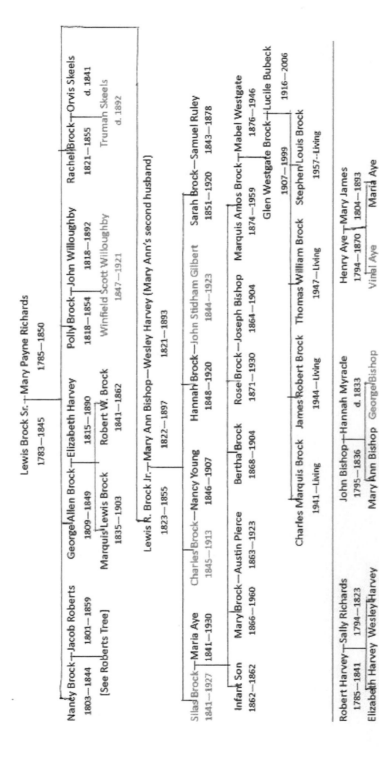

Brock, Harvey, Bishop, and Aye Family Trees (Partial)

NOTE: The seven men highlighted in red served in the Union army during the Civil War.

Appendix 2

Roberts Family and Friends—Purchases of Ash Grove Public Domain Land, 1834–1855

PURCHASER	RELATIONSHIP(S)	TOTAL ACREAGE/DATE(S)/(SECTION NO[S].)
Lewis Roberts (1780–1848)	Brother of Bishop Roberts	280 acres/1834, 1836, 1837 (28)
John Hunnel (1799–1865)	Relative of Lewis Roberts's wife Margaret Hunnel	200 acres/1834, 1836 (28, 29)
Bishop Robert Richford Roberts (1778–1843)	Brother of Lewis Roberts	200 acres/1835, 1836 (27, 28, 29)
Thomas Hawkins (c. 1805–1843)	Son-in-law of Lewis Roberts First husband of Matilda Roberts	183 acres/1835, 1839 (19)
John Nunamaker (1798–1876)	Son-in-law of Lewis Roberts Husband of Catharine Roberts	120 acres/1835, 1841? (19, 29, 30)
John Henry (d. 1865)	From Lawrence County, IN	80 acres/1836 (24)
Sarah Roberts Skeels (b. c. 1814)	Daughter of Lewis Roberts	80 acres/1837, 1838 (27)
Jacob Roberts (1801–1859)	Son of Lewis Roberts Husband of Nancy BROCK (sister of Lewis R. Brock Jr.)	63 acres/1837 (19)
Samuel Wesley Jenkins (1816–1851)	From Lawrence County, IN	58 acres/1838 (6 in what is now Fountain Creek Twp but was then in Ash Grove)
Lewis Roberts Jr. (1811–1895)	Son of Lewis Roberts	80 acres/1841 (21)

John Roberts (?)	Son of Lewis Roberts	80 acres/1841 (28)
George Nunamaker (1827–1904)	Son of John Nunamaker and Catharine Roberts	80 acres/1841 (20)
Catharine Roberts (1803–1873)	Daughter of Lewis Roberts Wife of John Nunamaker	40 acres/1842 (19)
Robert R. Roberts (1820–1872)	Son of Lewis Roberts	See below*
Alonzo Taylor (c. 1803–1885)	From Lawrence County, IN*	200 acres/ 1847, 1852, 1853 (13, 24) (additional purchase in 1864)
John Martin (b. c 1817)	Husband of Elizabeth Roberts (daughter of Lewis Roberts)	120 acres/1847, 1853 (21, 28)
John H. Stidham (?)	Son-in-law of Lewis Roberts Second husband of Matilda Roberts	280 acres/1849, 1853 (19, 34) (additional purchases in 1866)
John Willoughby (1818–1892)	Friend of Roberts family Husband of Polly BROCK (sister of Lewis R. Brock Jr.)	160 acres /1849, 1853 (27, 33) (additional purchases between 1869 and 1874)
James Q. Roberts (1826–1865)	Son of Jacob Roberts and Nancy BROCK	40 acres/1850 (27)
Robert Roberts Chess (1816–1871)	Son of Priscilla Roberts (sister of Lewis Roberts) and James Chess	240 acres/1852, 1853, 1855 (27, 33) (additional purchase in 1863)
Lewis Nunamaker (1836–1888)	Son of John Nunamaker and Catharine Roberts	160 acres/1853 (17)
Joseph Hawkins (1808–1864)	Husband of Ellenor Chess (daughter of James Chess and Priscilla	160 acres/1854 (26)

	Roberts)	
	TOTAL ACREAGE	**2,904 acres**

*Lewis Roberts died in February 1848. In June of that year, eight of his nine children transferred their interests in 160 acres in Section 28 that was part of his estate to the ninth and youngest child, Robert R. Roberts. I have included the latter as a member of the colony, but obviously, the total colony acreage did not increase because of his acquisition.

Appendix 3

Extended Brock Family—Purchases of Ash Grove Public Domain Land from the Government and of Land from the Illinois Central Railroad, 1836–1854

PURCHASER	RELATIONSHIP(S)	TOTAL ACREAGE/DATE(S)/SECTION NO(S).
Lewis Brock Sr. (1783–1845)	Father of Nancy Brock, George Allen Brock, Polly Brock, and Lewis R. Brock Jr. Grandfather of SILAS BROCK	160 acres/1836, 1838, 1839 (15 in Artesia; 23 in Ash Grove)
George Allen Brock (1809–1849)	Son of Lewis Brock Sr. Brother of Nancy Brock, Polly Brock, and Lewis R. Brock Jr Husband of Elizabeth Harvey Uncle of SILAS BROCK	343 acres/1837, 1838 (19, 23, 30)
Elizabeth Harvey (1815–1890)	Brother of Wesley Harvey Wife of George Allen Brock Aunt of SILAS BROCK	62 acres/1842 (30)
Lewis R. Brock Jr. (1823–1855)	Son of Lewis Brock Sr.	582 acres/1850, 1852, 1853, 1854 (3 in Loda; 25, 29, 30 in Ash Grove)

	Brother of Nancy Brock, George Allen Brock, and Polly Brock	
	Husband of Mary Ann Bishop	
	Father of SILAS BROCK	
Wesley Harvey (1821–1893)	**Brother of Elizabeth Harvey**	**160 acres/1852, 1853, 1854 (25)**
Silas Bishop (1820–1899)	**Brother of Mary Ann Bishop** **Uncle of SILAS BROCK**	**80 acres/1854 (35)**
	TOTAL ACREAGE	**1,387 acres**

Appendix 4

Pitchin Cemetery

Buried in Pitchin Cemetery are several members of the extended Roberts family and friends, including the following:

Lewis Roberts
Margaret Hunnel
John T. Roberts
Mary Temple
John Hunnel
Jane Hunnel
Thomas Hawkins
John H. Stidham
Matilda Roberts
John Willoughby
Polly Brock (John Willoughby's wife)
Joseph Hawkins
Ellenor Chess
John Shroyer
Samuel Wesley Jenkins

Also a number of Silas's extended family members, including the following:

Father Lewis R. Brock ("Lewis Jr.")
Mother Mary Ann Bishop
Grandfather Lewis Brock ("Lewis Sr.")
Sister Hannah Mary Brock (or Onarga Cemetery?)
Brother-in-law John Gilbert (Hannah Brock's husband) (or
        Onarga Cemetery?)
Uncle George Allen Brock
Aunt Polly Brock
Uncle John Willoughby (Polly Brock's husband)
Aunt Nancy Brock (wife of Jacob Roberts)
Uncle Henry Bishop (Mary Ann Bishop's brother)
Aunt Matilda Nunamaker (Henry Bishop's wife)
Aunt Phebe Aye (wife of Amos Bishop; sister of Maria
        Aye)
Aunt Elizabeth Jane Stedham (wife of Amos Bishop)
Niece Letty Bell Brock (daughter of Silas's brother Charles)
Brother-in-law Samuel Ruley (Sarah Brock's husband)
Stepfather Wesley Harvey
Wesley Harvey's first wife, Mary Henry

Appendix 5

Silas Brock's Relatives in Indiana Regiments

Following are brief summaries of the service records of Silas's three relatives who served in Indiana regiments:

Vinal Aye and the 31st Indiana, Company A. On September 5, 1861, Silas's brother-in-law, Vinal Aye, enlisted at age twenty-two as a private at Terre Haute, Indiana, in the 31st Regiment, Indiana Infantry, Company A. He was promoted to corporal shortly thereafter. In April 1863, he was promoted to sergeant. Then, in January 1864, Aye reenlisted as a veteran volunteer at Bridgeport, Alabama, and he was promptly promoted to sergeant. In 1865, he was promoted to first sergeant, then to first lieutenant, and finally to captain. Aye was mustered out on December 8, 1865, after more than four years of service.

John L. Roberts and the 117th Indiana, Company H or D. John L. Roberts, a first cousin of Silas's (the son of Jacob Roberts and Nancy Brock), enrolled for six months at age thirty-two in Bedford, Lawrence County, Indiana, in the 117th Indiana Volunteer Infantry Regiment on July 16, 1863. He was mustered in on August 19 at Indianapolis as a sergeant and mustered out at Indianapolis on February 24, 1864. His service record says he was a member of Company H, but the following website puts him in Company D, in which all the soldiers were from Lawrence County: http://www.civilwarindex.com/armyin/soldiers/117th_in_infantry_soldiers.pdf According to that website, all the soldiers in Company H were from Jackson County.

Lewis Roberts Shroyer and the 66th Indiana, Company A. Lewis Roberts Shroyer was the son of Matilda Roberts and John Shroyer, both natives of Washington County, Indiana. He was the grandson of Nancy Brock and Jacob Roberts, and thus Silas's first cousin once removed. His parents migrated to Ash Grove when they married, and Lewis was born there in 1841. However, his father died in 1846, and his mother then returned to Washington County.

On August 19, 1862, Shroyer was mustered into the 66th Indiana Regiment Volunteer Infantry, Company A, as a private at New Albany, Indiana for three years . On August 30, he was wounded in the left knee at the battle of Richmond, Kentucky, captured by the Confederates, but paroled. He was absent from his regiment because of his wound until June 1863, and he rejoined the regiment at Corinth, Mississippi in July.

Shroyer was put on "detached service" in the ambulance corps beginning July 15 until June 3, 1865, when he was mustered out at Washington, DC.

Appendix 6

Ash Grove Men in Illinois Regiments Other Than the 76th Illinois

25th Illinois, Company F. Eight Ash Grove men, including seven farmers and one engineer, joined the 25th Illinois Volunteer Infantry Regiment, Company F, in June 1861, for three years. Cpl. Morris Neighbor was killed in action at Pea Ridge, Arkansas, on March 8, 1862.

12th Illinois, Company C. Two Ash Grove farmers joined Company C of the 12th Illinois Volunteer Infantry Regiment for three years. Thomas Cady joined on September 8, 1861. The other joined later, in February 1864. Cady was the son of John and Ellen Cady. From March through June 1862, Cady was absent from his regiment, sick in the hospital in Paducah, Kentucky. He died of a severe gunshot wound in the thigh at City General Hospital in St. Louis, Missouri, on November 13, 1862. He had received the wound at the battle of Corinth, Mississippi, on October 4, 1862.

113th Illinois, Company D. Silas's uncle, George Bishop, another farmer from Ash Grove, enlisted at age thirty-eight on August 12 for three years. He was assigned to the 113th Illinois Volunteer Infantry Regiment, Company D. Bishop was a veteran of the Mexican War—private, 5th Regiment, Company C, from October 1847 to July 1848. Six other Ash Grove farmers also joined the 113th Illinois, Company D, for three years. That group included Truman Skeels, a first cousin of Silas's (the son of Orvis Skeels and Rachel Brock), who was court-martialed, as described in chapter 9. One of those men, David Swank, died of disease at Onarga, Illinois, on October 2, just one day after the regiment was mustered in.

134th Illinois, Company B. Nine Ash Grove men, including eight farmers and one printer, joined Company B of the 134th Illinois Volunteer Infantry Regiment in May 1864, for one hundred days. They spent those one hundred days in Columbus, Kentucky.

150th Illinois, Company D. Six Ash Grove farmers joined the 150th Illinois Volunteer Infantry Regiment, Company D, in February 1865 for one year. One of those was the son of John Willoughby and Polly Brock, eighteen-year-old Winfield Scott Willoughby, named for the famous general, and a first cousin of Silas.

58th Illinois, Company H. Finally, one Ash Grove farmer joined the 58th Illinois Volunteer Infantry Regiment Consolidated, Company H, in March 1865 for one year.

Bibliography

SOURCES

Abraham Lincoln, By Some Men Who Knew Him (1910). Bloomington, IL: Pantagraph Printing & Stationery Co., 1910, 111-112, 138-139.

Andrews, Brevet Major-General C. C. *History of the Campaign of Mobile*. New York: D. Van Nostrand Co., 2nd ed., 1889, 204-205.

Archives of DePauw University and Indiana United Methodism, Greencastle, Indiana. *Catalogue of the Officers and Students of the Indiana Asbury University for the Academical Year 1856-7.*

Archives of the Iroquois County Genealogical Society, Watseka, Illinois.   Various 19th-century files, including select files from the "Old Blue Cases," Grantor-Grantee Index, Iroquois County Original Land Purchases 1831-1882, Obituary Collection, and Iroquois County, IL Probate.

Atlas Map Iroquois County, Illinois. Edwardsville, IL: W. R. Brink & Co., 1884.   Part of *Combined Illustrated Atlas of Iroquois County, Illinois: 1884-1904-1921*.   Watseka, IL: Iroquois County Genealogical Society.

Beckwith, H. W. *History of Iroquois County, Together with Historic Notes on the Northwest.* Chicago, IL: H. H. Hill and Company, 1880.   I refer to this book throughout as the "Beckwith *History*" or "Beckwith."

> Public Land Survey System map of Ash Grove Township, Part I, page 260.
> Iroquois County in the War of the Great Rebellion, by Alex. L. Whitehall, Part I, pages 261-330.
> Pvt. Sylvanus Cass Munhall's letter to his newspaper, Part I, pages 287-288.
> First Lt. Peter Williams, Part I, pages 324-325.
> The story of Gurdon Hubbard and Noel Vasseur, Part I, pages 334-336.
> Relocation of the county seat of Iroquois County, Part I, page 351.
> Franklin Blades, Part I, page 442-444; Part II, page 65, 67.
> Removal of Indians, Part II, page 133.
> John Hunnel, Part I, pages 337-338; Part II, page 644.
> Ash Grove Township, Part II, pages 640-671.
> John Willoughby, Part II, page 642.
> Anecdote about Abraham Lincoln and Lewis Roberts, Part II, page 643.
> The story of how Ash Grove got its name, Part II, pages 641-642.
> John Nunamaker's pottery business, Part II, page 644.
> James Chess, Part II, pages 645 and 653.
> The trip from Ash Grove to Chicago, Part II, pages 647-648.
> The story of John Cady, Part II, pages 645-646.

Presidential election of 1840, Part II, page 649.
Lewis Roberts as justice of the peace, Part II, page 650.
Pitchin Cemetery, Part II, page 653.
The story of how Pitchin got its name, Part II, page 658.
The story of the two Methodist chapels, Part II, pages 654-655.
Wesley Harvey, Part II, pages 661-662.

Blackstock, Towner (Curator of Archives). *The Archives of Phi Gamma Delta. Lambda Chapter at Indiana Asbury: Initiates, 1856-1870.* December 2006. http://www.phigam.org/b9-pages/about/history/indianalambda. These archives include a photograph and biography of Marquis Lewis Brock, a cousin of Silas Brock. Mr. Blackstock kindly provided me with a higher-resolution photograph for inclusion in this story. See Chapter 13.

Cissna Park, Illinois: 1882-1982. Cissna Park, IL: Cissna Park Centennial Corporation, 1982. Quotation from Doris Kogler, at page 90.

Claytonville Centennial 1882-1982. Silas Brock, 36.

Dowling, John. *History of Iroquois County 1818-1968.* Watseka, IL: Iroquois County Board of Supervisors, 1968.

Eddy, T. M. *The Patriotism of Illinois: A Record of the Civil and Military History of the State in the War for the Union.* Chicago, IL: Clarke & Co., 1865. Adjutant-General Fuller's Report – 1:125-127. Meridian Campaign – 2:160-165.

Find A Grave. http://www.findagrave.com. Family history and genealogy of the Roberts family.

Fraser, Clayton B. (Creator). "Detail of 76th Illinois Volunteer Infantry Regiment Memorial, Section 1. View to Northeast.—Mobile National Cemetery, 1202 Virginia Street, Mobile, Mobile County, AL" Photograph, Historic American Buildings Survey. Fraserdesign, 2006. From Library of Congress: *Prints and Photographs Division,* HABS AL-1-25. http://www.loc.gov/pictures/resource/hhh.al1321.photos.364464p/.

Frazer, Todd M. *One Hundred Years of Learning at Grand Prairie Seminary and Onarga Military School, 1863-1963.* Onarga, IL: Onarga Military School, 1963. https://archive.org/details/onehundredyearso00fraz\.

Garfield, Jannette (Transcriber). *1860 Federal Census of Iroquois County, Illinois.* Sponsored by the Iroquois County Genealogical Society.

Gocken, Cheryl (Compiler). *1830 Vermilion Co. Census; 1840 Iroquois Co. Census with Index.* Evansville, IN: Evansville Bindery, Inc., 1992. Sponsored by the Iroquois County Genealogical Society.

Grierson's route from La Grange to Baton Rouge.... Map. Harper's new monthly magazine, v. 27, June-November 1863, page 271. From Library of Congress, *Geography and Map Division. http://www.loc.gov/item/99447404/.*

Historic Memphis--Irving Block Prison.
http://historic-memphis.com/memphis/irving-block/irving-block.html
By email dated December 5, 2015, the webmaster of that website advised me that the report to President Lincoln regarding the prison is in the public domain. See also https://ehistory.osu.edu/books/official-records/120/0404.

Illinois Secretary of State. *Illinois State Archives: Illinois Adjutant General's Report: Regimental and Unit Histories.*
https://www.cyberdriveillinois.com/departments/archives/databases/reghist.pdf

Illinois Secretary of State. *Illinois State Archives: Illinois Civil War Muster and Descriptive Rolls.*
http://www.cyberdriveillinois.com/departments/archives/databases/datcivil.html

Illinois Secretary of State. *Illinois State Archives: Illinois Public Domain Land Tract Sales.*
http://www.cyberdriveillinois.com/departments/archives/databases/data_lan.html.

Iroquois County Cemetery Project: Ash Grove Twp. Cemeteries. Watseka, IL: Iroquois County Genealogical Society, 1995.

Iroquois County History. Watseka, IL: Iroquois County Historical Society, 1985. Silas and Maria (Aye) Brock, 195-196.

Journal of the House of Representatives of the State of Illinois: Eleventh General Assembly, First Session (1838). Vandalia, IL: William Walters, 1838.
https://archive.org/details/journalofhouseof01eilli.

Journal of the House of Representatives of the State of Illinois: Eleventh General Assembly, Second Session (1839-1840). Springfield, IL: W. Walters, 1840.
https://archive.org/details/journalofhouseof1839illi.

Journal of the House of Representatives of the State of Indiana: Eleventh Session of the General Assembly (1826-1827). Indianapolis, IN: John Douglas.
https://ia600300.us.archive.org/25/items/journalofhouseof182627indi/journalofhouseof182627indi.pdf.

Kern, J. W. *Past and Present of Iroquois County, Illinois.* Chicago, IL: S. J. Clarke Publishing Co., 1907.

    Biographical sketch of Silas Brock, pages 537-539.
    Biographical sketch of Wesley Harvey, pages 422-424.

Maj. Matthew H. Peters's description of the Confederate defenses at Fort Blakely, page 692.

Landes, Tylla Herman. "The Early History of Cissna Park, Illinois." See chapter 12. Unpublished undated manuscript in Glen Brock's files.

"Lawrence County, Indiana: First Land Owners." http://www.ingenweb.org/inlawrence/owners/index.htm.

Laws of the State of Illinois—The Eleventh General Assembly. "An act to relocate the seat of justice of the county of Iroquois." Vandalia: William Walters, 1839, 185-187. https://archive.org/details/lawsofstateofill11illi

Map of Kentucky and Tennessee. Map. Century illustrated monthly magazine, vol. 34, August 1887. From Library of Congress, *Geography and Map Division*. http://www.loc.gov/item/99447354/.

Map of Iroquois County (Current). https://en.wikipedia.org/wiki/Iroquois_County,_Illinois. Created by Omnedon.

Miller, Mary J. (Compiler). *1850 Census of Iroquois County, Illinois with Index*. Watseka, IL: Iroquois County Genealogical Society, 1979.

Moore, Ralph D., and Virginia M. Moore. *Iroquois County Original Land Purchases 1831-1882*. Watseka, IL: Iroquois County Historical Society, 1977. The Iroquois County Geneological Society advised me by email dated December 14, 2015 that this book was given to it many years ago, and that I may use what I need from the book.

Portrait and Biographical Record of Iroquois County, Illinois, Containing Biographical Sketches of Prominent and Representative Citizens. Chicago, IL: Lake City Publishing Co., 1893.

Description of Iroquois County in 1833, pages 641-642.
Biographical sketch of Silas Brock, pages 641-643.
Biographical sketch of Wesley Harvey, pages 422-424.
Biographical sketch of Amos Bishop, pages 572-575.
Biographical sketch of Austin Pierce, pages 612-613.

Proceedings of the Reunions of the Society of Survivors of the 76th Regiment Illinois Infantry (1886-1911, excluding 1893, 1896, 1897, 1910, 1911, and subsequent reunions). Watseka, IL: *Watseka Republican Book Print*.

1st Reunion, Kankakee, IL, October 27-28, 1886
2nd Reunion, Watseka, IL, October 5-6, 1887
3rd Reunion, Morris, IL, October 10-11, 1888
4th Reunion, Urbana, IL, September 4-5, 1889

5th Reunion, Momence, IL, October 2-3, 1890
6th Reunion, Kankakee, IL, October 7-8, 1891
7th Reunion, Watseka, IL October 11-12, 1892
[No reunion held in 1893]
8th Reunion, Sheldon, IL, October 10-11, 1894
9th Reunion, Watseka, IL, October 9-10, 1895
[10th and 11th Reunions—proceedings not located]
12th Reunion, Urbana, IL, October 12-13, 1898
13th Reunion, Kankakee, IL, October 11-12, 1899
14th Reunion, Watseka, IL, October 10-11, 1900
15th Reunion, Kankakee, IL, October 9-10, 1901
16th Reunion, Momence, IL, October 8-9, 1902
17th Reunion, Urbana, IL, October 7-8, 1903
18th Reunion, Watseka, IL, October 11-12, 1904
19th Reunion, Kankakee, IL, October 11-12, 1905
20th Reunion, Momence, IL, October 10-11, 1906
21st Reunion, Urbana, IL, October 9-10, 1907
22nd Reunion, Watseka, IL, October 7-8, 1908
23rd Reunion, Kankakee, IL, October 13-14, 1909
[24th Reunion—proceedings not located]
25th Reunion, Urbana, IL, October 11-12, 1911
    [only notice of reunion located]
[Subsequent reunions—proceedings not located.
According to the *Kankakee Daily Republican* of
October 13, 1921, a reunion was held there at
that time. That information was provided by
Doris Kogler.]

Ridpath, Martha J., ed. *Alumnal Record, DePauw University*. Greencastle, IN: DePauw University, 1920, 22, 380, and 522.

Sneden, Robert Knox. *Rebel defences [sic] of Mobile shewing [sic} Union attack April 3rd-9th 1865 on Spanish Fort*. Map. Robert Knox Sneden diary, 1865. Repository: Virginia Historical Society. On Library of Congress website. http://www.loc.gov/item/gvhs01.vhs00201/. The Virginia Historical Society advised me by email dated January 5, 2016, that I have permission to use this map.

The Seat of War on the Mississippi. Map. Harper's new monthly magazine, v. 27, June-November 1863, page 271. On the verso of "*Grierson's route from La Grange to Baton Rouge.*" From Library of Congress, *Geography and Map Division*. *http://www.loc.gov/item/99447404/* .

Tippy, Worth Marion. *Frontier Bishop: The Life and Times of Robert Richford Roberts 1778—1843*. New York, NY: Abingdon Press, 1958. By email dated December 11, 2015, the United Methodist Publishing House advised me that the copyright on this work was allowed to lapse, and that the book is in the public domain.

Tomlinson, George W. *New Map of Vicksburg.* Map. Boston, J. Mayer & Co., lith., c. 1863. From Library of Congress, *Geography and Map Division.* http://www.loc.gov/resource/g3984v.cw0286000/.

United States Army Corps of Engineers. *Rebel line of works at Blakely captured by the Army of West Miss., April 9, 1865: Position & approaches by the Union forces.* Map. Engineer Dept., 1865. From Library of Virginia Map Collection, Richmond, VA. Included in this story by permission.

United States Census Bureau, Illinois County Selection Map, http://quickfacts.census.gov/qfd/maps/illinois_map.html. Used for County Identification.

United States Census Bureau, Indiana County Selection Map, http://quickfacts.census.gov/qfd/maps/indiana_map.html. Used for County Identification.

United States Department of the Interior, Bureau of Land Management. *General Land Office Records.* http://www.glorecords.blm.gov/search/default.aspx. Information regarding federal land patents.

United States National Archives. *Veterans Service Records.* http://www.archives.gov/veterans/.

   Vinal Aye, 31st Ind., Co. A
   George Bishop, 113th Ill., Co. D
   Surgeon Franklin Blades, 76th Ill.
   Benjamin Bratton, 76th Ill., Co. E
   Elijah Bratten, 76th Ill., Co. K
   Charles Brock, 76th Ill., Co. E
   Silas Brock, 76th Ill., Co. E
   Col. Samuel T. Busey, 76th Ill.
   Thomas P. T. Cady, 12th Ill., Co. C
   James Wesley Chess, 12th Ind., Co. A
   Jonathan G. Clawson, 76th Ill., Co. K
   Isaac Courtright, 76th Ill., Co. I
   Ferdinand Foucaud, 76th Ill., Co. F
   William Gasaway, 67th Ind., Co. H
   John S. Gilbert, 76th Ill., Co. K
   Maj. George C. Harrington, 76th Ill.
   Hiram Harris, 76th Ill., Co. K
   Elisha Hawkins, 76th Ill., Co. K
   James Higginson, 76th Ill., Co. E
   Capt. Henry W. B. Hoyt, 113th Ill., Co. A
   Capt. Richard Hughes, 76th Ill., Co. C
   Henry B. Hussey, 76th Ill., co. K
   Capt. Abram Irvin, 76th Ill., Co. E
   Lt. Col. Charles C. Jones, 76th Ill.

William F. Kenaga, 76th Ill., Co. I
Harvey B. Longnecker, 76th Ill., Co. E
Michael Lovett, 113th Ill., Co. D
Joseph B. McKinley, 76th Ill., Co. E
Chaplain John W. Monser, 76th Ill.
Samuel W. Montgomery, 76th Ill., Co. E
Aaron Moore, 115th Ohio, Co. F
Sylvanus C. Munhall, 76th Ill., Co. B
Oliver Nail, 76th Ill., Co. K
Morris Neighbor, 25th Ill., Co. F
John W. Nunamaker, 84th Ill., Co. F
John L. Roberts, 117th Ind., Co. D
Thomas H. Roberts, 76th Ill., Co. K
Samuel T. Rowley, 76th Ill., Co. K
Aaron Russell, 76th Ill., Co. K
Lewis Roberts Shroyer, 66th Ind., Co. A
John W. Shuck, 76th Ill., Co. B
Orvis Skeels, 57th Ill., Co. C
Truman H. Skeels, 113th Ill., Co. D (including Court-Martial
     Case File #LL-2585)
Hamilton Spain, 76th Ill., Co. E
James B. Spain, 33rd Iowa, Co. C
John Spain, 134th Ill., Co. B
John W. Spain, 174th Ohio, Co. C
Moses Spain, 76th Ill., Co. E
George W. Thomas, 76th Ill., Co. K
Isaac C. VanHorn, 76th Ill., Co. K
Joel L. Vaughn, 76th Ill., Co. K
Winfield Scott Willoughby, 150th Ill., Co. D
William H. Wilson, 113th Ill., Co. D; 120th Ill., Co. H

United States National Park Service. *The Civil War—Battle Unit Details—United States Colored Troops—66th Regiment, United States Colored Infantry.* http://www.nps.gov/civilwar/search-battle-units-detail.htm?battleUnitCode=UUS0066RI00C.

United States National Park Service. *Vicksburg National Military Park, Mississippi—Illinois Memorial.* http://www.nps.gov/vick/historyculture/illinois-memorial.htm)

United States National Park Service. *Vicksburg National Military Park, Mississippi—76th Illinois Infantry.* http://www.nps.gov/vick/learn/historyculture/76th-illinois-infantry.htm.

Walton, Clyde C. *Illinois and the Civil War.* Springfield, IL: Civil War Centennial Commission of Illinois, 1961, 19. Walton was an Illinois State historian.

WBIW.com. "Cavetown Cemetery Board Meeting and Pitch-In Sept. 28." September 22, 2014.
http://www.wbiw.com/local/archive/2014/09/cavetown-cemetery-board-meeting-and-pitch-in-sept-28.php.

CIVIL WAR SONGS

"We Are Coming, Father Abraham" (chapter 8):
Irving, A. B. (composer) Sheet music. Chicago: H. M. Higgins, 1862. From Library of Congress, Music Division. http://www.loc.gov/item/ihas.200001455/.

"The Battle Cry of Freedom" (chapter 8):
Root, George F. (composer). Sheet music. Chicago: Root & Cady, 1862. From Library of Congress, Music Division. http://www.loc.gov/item/ihas.200001814/.

"Tenting on the Old Camp Ground" (chapter 9):
Kittredge, Walter (composer and lyricist). Sheet music. Boston: Oliver Ditson & Co., 1864. From Library of Congress, Music Division.
http://www.loc.gov/item/ihas.200001502/.

"The Vacant Chair" (chapter 11):
Root, George F. (composer), Henry Stevenson Washburn (lyricist). Sheet music. Cincinnati, OH: John Church Co., 1862. From Library of Congress, Music Division.
http://www.loc.gov/item/ihas.100008719/.

SOURCES NOT EXAMINED

For possible future reference, following are two items related to the 76th Illinois Volunteer Infantry Regiment that I have identified but not yet examined:

Busey, Samuel T. *Diary, 1865 Feb. 16 to 1865 Apr. 23.*
https://www.worldcat.org/title/diary-1865-feb-16-to-1865-apr-23/oclc/70956540&referer=brief_results.
Identified as being located at the University of West Florida John C. Pace Library, Pensacola, Florida.

Eastburn, James H. *Diary, 1862-1865.* https://www.worldcat.org/title/diary-1862-1865/oclc/17725249&referer=brief_results.
Identified as being located at the Western Reserve Historical Society Research Library, Cleveland, Ohio. By letter dated January 9, 2015, the Library staff advised me that the diary does not contain any photographs of Silas Brock.

Made in the USA
Lexington, KY
26 February 2019